2.50
1/25

ATTACHMENT AND
NEW BEGINNINGS

Other titles in the UKCP Series:

ATTACHMENT AND NEW BEGINNINGS

Reflections on Psychoanalytic Therapy

Jonathan Pedder

Edited by

Gary Winship

On behalf of the United Kingdom Council
for Psychotherapy

KARNAC

First published in 2010 by
Karnac Books Ltd
118 Finchley Road, London NW3 5HT

British Library Cataloguing in Publication Data

A C.I.P. for this book is available from the British Library

ISBN: 978 1 85575 632 8

Edited, designed and produced by The Studio Publishing Services Ltd
www.publishingservicesuk.co.uk
e-mail: studio@publishingservicesuk.co.uk

Printed in Great Britain

www.karnacbooks.com

CONTENTS

ACKNOWLEDGEMENTS

A few years after I had retired from the Maudsley Hospital, a former psychotherapy supervisee, Gary Winship, approached me with the idea that a collection of some of my papers could be useful. We discussed this, and in due course agreed which papers might form a coherent whole. Since then, Gary has tirelessly pursued this project and put in a great deal of work and effort, for which I am very grateful.

It will be clear from these papers that certain analysts have greatly influenced my thinking on many psychoanalytic issues. The most significant have been Balint, Bowlby, and Winnicott. There are others (some sadly now dead) with whom I have discussed ideas at length over the years and these include Nina Coltart, Wally Joffe, John Klauber, Adam Limentani, and Vera Pettitt. I cannot overestimate their influence and the help they have given me. Others include Dennis Brown, with whom I co-authored our book in 1979, which Antony Bateman has turned into the third and fourth editions. I also single out three groups: those with whom I went to Denmark to train their psychoanalysts in psychoanalytic psychotherapy; those psychoanalysts with whom I travelled to try to extend psychoanalysis beyond London; and, finally, those from the

Maudsley who attended my weekly seminars over the years, which provoked many interesting ideas and was mutually enriching.

I must also thank Karnac for their support, guidance, and persistence in getting this book off the ground. They have given much helpful advice from beginning to the end.

Finally, I thank my family for their support over the years, and especially my wife, whose help in this project has been invaluable, particularly her work as translator, interpreter, and intermediary with Gary during my recent illness.

Jonathan Pedder
December 2009

ABOUT THE AUTHOR AND EDITOR

Jonathan Pedder was formerly Consultant Psychotherapist at the Maudsley Hospital, a member of the British Psychoanalytic Society, founder member of the Association of Psychoanalytic Psychotherapy in the NHS (APP), and is co-author, with Dennis Brown, of *Introduction to Psychotherapy* (now in its 4th edition). Pedder was instrumental in the development of public sector psychotherapy from the early years of the "Rugby" conference on psychotherapy as a representative for the Royal College of Psychiatrists, and then as a council member for the UK Standing Conference for psychotherapy. As a writer, teacher, clinician, and supervisor, his clinical application of the independent tradition of Bowlby, Winnicott, and Balint has been one of the most highly regarded contributions of a generation.

Gary Winship, PhD, MA, RMN, Dip Gp Psych, Cert Add, is a UKCP registered psychotherapist, NMC MHN registered, Associate Professor, School of Education, University of Nottingham. He is a Senior Fellow of the Institute of Mental Health, and was formerly Senior Adult Psychotherapist, Berkshire NHS Trust, Broadmoor & Maudsley Hospitals. Winship began working in a National Health

Service (NHS) psychotherapeutic community at the Bethlem Royal Hospital in 1980. He became a CHI reviewer in 2000, and he continues to consult to the NHS regarding the advancement of psychological therapies. Currently course leader for the MA in Counselling Children & Young People, University of Nottingham, he is a busy tutor, clinical and PhD supervisor, practitioner, and researcher. He is currently developing a clinical doctorate in psychotherapy.

Foreword

Jeremy Holmes, University of Exeter

> "The noblest therapist of them all ... We all have much to
> learn from this reticent master of our discipline, and I am
> sure this book, like its subject, will evoke the admiration,
> affection, and respect it deserves
>
> (Jeremy Holmes on Jonathan Pedder)

Psychoanalysis has no lack of eponymous heroes (the founder himself and his daughter, Jung, Klein, Lacan, and Kohut, among others), each of whom represents a rallying point for a faction of our fractious discipline. But unhappy the age that has need of heroes, and three cheers for the unsung, of whom Jonathan Pedder is an outstanding example.

Pedder's unique contribution, intrinsic to his modesty, is his capacity to remain loyal to the contradictory British blend of empiricism, romanticism, and democracy, while fully embracing the startling originality of the psychoanalytic *weltanshaung*. Almost all his contributions are imbued with this spirit, whether arguing the case for psychoanalysis as an integral part of psychiatry, the need for simple human contact as well as interpretation in the consulting room, for a developmental account of depression that takes account of real trauma, or for parallels between catharsis in therapy and theatre.

Psychotherapeutic politics

I first met Jonathan when he was Chair of the Psychotherapy faculty of the Royal College of Psychiatrists. He was by far the best Chair among the many I served under. One was immediately struck by his uprightness, both physical and moral: a man of total integrity, a good listener yet able to stick to his principles, combining an enviable overview of strategy with attention to minute detail of phraseology, spelling, and punctuation. (It was from him that I learned that invaluable committee technique—in his case an aspect of his conscientiousness—of homing in on typos embedded in dense documents, thereby outflanking the majority of committee members, who habitually give papers little more than a cursory glance.) An enthusiastic sailor in his spare time, one knew one would be in utterly safe hands with him at the helm.

Jonathan's reticence, together with what I perceive as his instinctive aversion to the narcissistic lure of leadership, meant that he was more monarch-maker than king, the power behind the throne rather than incumbent. But, although by nature cautious, he knew when to press home his point without deflection. At a coffee-fuelled cabal where the plot was hatched to establish the first psychotherapist President of the College, the turning point came with Jonathan's quoting from Julius Caesar, "there is a tide in the affairs of men, which, taken at the flood . . .". He insisted that the time was ripe and that we should *carpe diem*—perhaps also revealing himself, Brutus-like, as the noblest therapist of them all.

The capacity to grasp the essential point, simplify it, and then look at its ramifications and implications, is to be found throughout his writings. Often he starts from an idea thrown out by one of his illustrious forebears—especially Balint and Winnicott—and develops it, clarifying and adding his own original twist. I imagine he is an excellent therapist. His capacity to listen intently to the "minute particulars" (Hobson, 1985), to get to the intellectual and emotional heart of the matter, to stick to his guns ("there is no such thing as peace time", one of his memorable aphorisms, applicable both to psychoanalytic politics and perhaps no less to the unremitting ambivalence of the analytic relationship) while remaining open and receptive, is the essence of good therapy.

His Whiggish aliveness to historical forces and the importance of enlightened leadership enables him to transcend the sometimes narrow confines of psychoanalytic thinking in the social and political arena (Chapter Seven). A passionate and eloquent advocate for psychoanalysis as a necessary component of all the helping professions, he is always ready to endorse eclectic approaches in which psychoanalytic ideas are adapted to clinical and political realities without losing their essential nature (Chapter Six).

Language

Pedder's theoretical contributions can, I believe, be traced to his ability both to pay intense attention to the minutiae of language, and, following Freud's railway metaphor, to follow wherever the words—as "switches" or junction points—take one, often in new and unexpected directions. Depending on context, he can stay reassuringly on track, or become enjoyably playful. Drawing on his natural balance and poise, he steers an even course through the ever-present analytic pitfalls of wildness and dogmatism. It is hard to imagine his vessel capsizing, or getting stuck in the doldrums.

In the remainder of this brief introduction to a long-overdue collection (for which we should be very grateful to Gary Winship), I pick out three of these linguistic pirouettes that I have found particularly illuminating, and then delineate some of the ways in which Pedder epitomizes the Independent voice in British psychoanalysis.

As far as I know, Pedder was the first to point out the etymological link between the words *metaphor* and *transference*, the former derived from the Greek, the latter from Latin, but both meaning "to carry over", or "bring across". Influenced by Winnicott, Pedder emphasizes the essential playfulness of the analytic relationship, and the importance of "learning to play" as a positive aspect of both process and outcome in therapy.

To enter metaphorical mode is to find deeper likenesses between apparently dissimilar things. The "work" of therapy (which in reality is more akin to "play") relies greatly on metaphor / simile (some of which are "dead" or conventional metaphors, some arising anew in the minds of the participants): "what does your depression feel *like* . . .?", "it sounds as though you sometimes are utterly *trapped* by your current role"; "listening to you made me think of someone *groping in the dark* with no reassuring hand to hold . . .".

Pedder's original insight was that transference itself is, via Matte-Blancoean symmetrization, a species of metaphor, finding parallels between the superficially very different situations of being a patient seeking help, and a child faced with parents towards whom he or she has a mixture of contradictory emotions. Thus, the "play" of therapy becomes utterly real as links with the past reveal themselves, and "reality" playfully mutable as the ways in which the assumptions and phantasies which colour and distort current perceptions are disclosed.

Staying with another linguistic association to the word "play" (Chapter One), Pedder likens therapy to the experience of theatre: the capacity of great works of the imagination, while bracketed off from reality, nevertheless to deepen our understanding of emotional and social life. Freud famously compared the analyst to a surgeon, cool, detached, opaque, able skilfully to wield the knife of interpretation in order to reveal and excise the offending psychopathology. Pedder switches—carries us across—from the operating theatre into the world of drama. He shows how the frame, analytic and theatrical, marks the boundary between the external and internal worlds; the similarity of cathartic immersion in emotional reality; the trajectory from uncertain beginnings, as the curtain rises or the session starts, to the emergence of themes, tensions, and their resolution; finally, at the end of the performance / session, the necessary return to "real life", with all its rewards and uncertainties.

A third example of the acuteness of Pedder's ear is his critique of Strachey's translation from the original as "Analysis terminable and interminable" in Freud's famous 1937 paper (Chapter Five). He points out that the English title could more accurately have been translated as "Psychoanalysis finite or infinite". The very different linguistic harmonics of that road not taken might have steered non-German speaking analysts away from the abortive or guillotine-like implications of termination and irritable ones of interminability, suggesting instead themes of separation, death, a timeless unconscious, and the infinity of irreversible loss. As always, Pedder thinks through the practical implications of ideas, in this case suggesting, as compared with classical technique, a more titrated, attenuated approach to ending, acknowledging the role of continuing "mature dependency" of patients on their analysts.

Independent thinking in psychoanalysis

A paradox of the Independent stream in psychoanalysis is that its very core values—suspicion of grand theories, valuation of the dialogic and the provisional—mean that it can appear to lack a clearly identified position or viewpoint. At its worst, the middle group appears to be a muddle group. Close reading of Pedder's oeuvre, made possible for the first time by this collection, counteracts this prejudice, and reveals the key features of Independent thought in an exemplary way.

I have already focused on Pedder's *sensitivity to language*, and his valuation of *play* as a crucial mutative element in the analytic relationship. To these, I would add several other aspects, which I see as central to the Independent tradition. First, the capacity to be *un-hidebound by tradition* and quasi-Talmudic adherence to the psychoanalytic canon. Pedder draws on Bowlby (Chapter Two), Fairbairn, and Balint to argue that attachment and non-sexual love (agape) are of equal importance to Eros and Thanatos as motivators in human affairs (cf. Holmes, 2009).

From this flows the capacity, indeed necessity, of *openness to relevant non-psychoanalytic research findings and ideas*, leading to cross-fertilization and hybrid vigour, rather than sterility and repetitiousness. A good example here is his discussion (Chapters Three and Four) of Brown's studies of depression in women and the finding that early loss of a parent predisposes to depression in later life. Pedder's inspired speculation that the age at which this occurs influences whether the subsequent depression is neurotic or psychotic in character has yet to be fully tested.

A third element is Pedder's ability to remain *in touch with "common sense"* while still drawing on analytic ideas. Indeed, it is this very capacity that makes him such a powerful ambassador for psychoanalysis among non-psychoanalytic colleagues, such as psychiatrists, and the non-psychoanalytic psychotherapists. He is multi-lingual, equally at home in the conceptual worlds of psycho-analysis, psychiatry, and medicine. His worry about the splitting off of the British Confederation of Psychotherapists psychoanalysts from the remainder of the psychotherapeutic community in UKCP (Chapters Six and Seven) reflects this concern for mutual under-standing and translation (another variant of metaphor/transfer-ence). "Pedder's rule" (Chapter Five)—the period of notice which a patient should be given of an impending ending of a therapy should be the square root of the number of months the patient has been in treatment—is a typically elegant nugget of clinical wisdom, but not, I suspect, to be found in the Collected Works of the Master.

Pedder (Chapter Six) draws on Balint's horticultural metaphor of "pruning" as a model for both supervision and for the role of the analyst in helping patients' emotional growth. This Anglo-Saxon, "Protestant" model can be contrasted with the more "Catholic" approaches to be found in some other psychoanalytic traditions. For Pedder, the role of the analyst is *"maieutic"* (cf. Scott, 2008), that of a midwife who does not wish to interpose herself between the patient and his unconscious, but helps shape, encourage, and facil-itate, and, when necessary, remove dead wood. Like Luther's God, the unconscious speaks directly to the subject in the Independent tradition, never via an omniscient analyst.

Finally the Independent tradition is unequivocally interper-sonal–relational, seeing *the therapeutic relationship as one between two human beings*. The contribution of the analyst is never fully reducible to technique. Important though transference and coun-tertransference, projective identification, drives, and defence are, there remain *au fond*, two human beings in a relationship, trying to understand one another and to find the support and succour that suffering calls forth. Winship (Chapter Seven) appositely questions Pedder's espousal of medical hegemony in the field of psychother-apy. But, paradoxically, Pedder's medical and psychiatric back-ground mean that he is able to see the simple humanity that lies behind roles and titles, the inescapability of human suffering, and the requirement, never fully realizable, to alleviate it.

In wrestling with these problems, Jonathan Pedder is an exem-plary un-hero (although never the anti-hero—his rebelliousness is always held well in check). As Winship elegantly puts it, he remains consistently "clear, precise, accurate, and engaging". We all have much to learn from this reticent master of our discipline, and I am sure this book, like its subject, will evoke the admiration, affection, and respect it deserves.

References

Hobson, R. F. (1985). *Forms of Feeling: the Heart of Psychotherapy*. London: Tavistock.

Holmes, J. (2009). *Exploring In Security: Towards an Attachment-informed Psychoanalytic Psychotherapy*. London: Routledge.

Scott, D. (Ed.) (2008). *Maieusis: Essays in Ancient Philosophy in Honour of Myles Burnyet*. Oxford: Oxford Scholarship Online.

Editor's introduction

Gary Winship

During the late 1980s, the Maudsley psychotherapy department was trying to embed psychoanalytic thinking across the hospital and became, to borrow one of Jonathan Pedder's metaphors (see Chapter Eight), "a lighthouse of excellence". I was involved in the psychotherapy department for several years, earlier working with Beatrice Stevens and Murray Jackson, and later for four years when Jonathan Pedder was my supervisor during my psychotherapy training. I recall the large psychotherapy department meetings and teaching sessions where there was one voice that seemed to rise quietly above the mêlée. In his Foreword here, Jeremy Holmes describes some of Jonathan's personal qualities of wisdom and diplomacy, which seem to have set him apart from those around him. I, too, came to admire Jonathan's qualities in meetings and then in individual supervision sessions I had with him, both during and then after my training was finished.

The idea of publishing a collection of Jonathan's papers was born out of the lasting value that I have found in reading them, and the usefulness many students of mine have also noted. Initially, I talked about the idea of publishing a collection of Jonathan's papers with Nick Temple, Anton Obholzer, and Bob Hinshelwood, among others, all of whom were very encouraging. Pippa Weitz and Karnac Books were receptive. In deciding which papers should be included, I had several discussions with Jonathan. It seemed important that the papers should reflect the natural cycle or process of therapy, starting from the beginnings (Jonathan writes eloquently about what happens in the opening moments of the drama of the session) through to the establishment of attachment, dependency, and transference. His best known paper on "endings" is included here, where Jonathan's recasts the idea of "termination" in analysis, suggesting that we might have a more upbeat notion with the idea of ending as a sort of "graduation", bringing to a close the clinical encounter. The cycle of therapy is brought full circle with further papers on the process of supervision and the organization and aspirations of psychoanalytic therapy itself in the public sphere.

In getting the papers together and re-editing them, some papers have been conflated. Jonathan's wife, Sue Pedder, has been exceptionally helpful and instrumental in realizing the project, as well as checking and sub-editing the papers herself. I have certainly valued talking with her about the context to some of the papers in terms of their history: for instance, I have learned that, along with Murray Jackson, Colin James, and Malcolm Pines, Jonathan worked on developing psychoanalysis in Denmark during the early 1980s.

Pippa Weitz said from the outset that it would be useful to have introductory comments on each chapter in order to contemporize them. I am particularly grateful to Dr Ronnie Doctor, Professor Del Lowenthal, Professor Bob Young, and Dr Melanie Bowden, who have all looked at different chapters and have given me feedback which has fed into my introductions. It is my hope that my introductions are not distracting, and that they convey something of the continuing value we might attach to the papers.

Professor Diane Waller, Professor Bob Hinshelwood, Dr Ronnie Doctor, and Mr Mike Brearley have all read final drafts of the book and have offered orientating endorsements of the book. Likewise, Jeremy Holmes read the draft of the book and has written a Foreword which expresses, better than I ever could, the deep appreciation that many of us feel towards Jonathan Pedder and his work.

It has been an absolute pleasure for me to be engaged in this project, an opportunity to say thank you to Jonathan in a way that I was not able to express during the time of being in supervision.

Sadly, Jonathan died earlier this year, shortly after the final draft of the book was finished. Sue tells me that he had known that the work was complete. His funeral was held at St Peter's Church in London, a moving occasion with many friends and colleagues, alongside Jonathan's family. This book is a timely celebration of Jonathan's significant contribution to the field of psychotherapy.

Gary Winship
June 2010

Commentary (GW)* on Chapter One: The role of space and location in psychotherapy, play, and theatre

T he start of therapy is framed as an initial encounter that might be considered in terms of the drama of a theatrical performance. Pedder compares the moment of the curtain-raising in the theatre with the opening moments in a therapy session. Both are experiences which are characterized by anxiety and anticipation, some of which is unavoidable, and some of which is necessary to achieve a level of focus. As one observes the drama unfold in the plot of a play, so the process of therapy begins to move towards a deeper encounter with the patient's internal world; the plot thickens, as they say. Pedder adopts a well-known quote from the New Testament; "through a glass, darkly" which is usually interpreted to mean that people have an imperfect perception of reality. The sentiments here are clear enough: that psychotherapy orientates a clearer grasp of reality for the client. But it is not in a cognitive or rational sense of orientating the client, rather, Pedder's idea is that it is through pleasure and play that we learn about the world, as we did in childhood and then onwards. The

---

*The commentaries that precede each chapter have been written by the editor, Gary Winship.

suspension of reality in drama and creative enterprise is the frame from which the role of play in psychotherapy is conceptualized.

Winnicott's (1971) ideas about potential space in *Playing and Reality* are mainstay here. There are resonances also of *The Drama of Being a Child*, by Alice Miller (1987), and *Theatres of the Mind*, by Joyce McDougall (1985). Pedder's assertion is that the role of drama and play in therapy is essential to fostering a milieu where creativity can flourish. In this day and age, where therapy has become increasingly businesslike, for instance, in cognitive–behaviour therapy (CBT), we do well to remember that many of our clients have lost the capacity to play, or may not have learnt it in the first place. How many current professional trainings in the field of mental health these days prepare practitioners with the requisite resources to foster creative potential space and play with clients? Moments of joy, relaxation, and play are as crucial to therapeutic progress as thinking and rationalization. Whereas some therapies today tend to exert exacting clinical procedures with manualized and measurable interventions, with "homework" to be completed at certain times by patients, Pedder reminds us that the intention of therapy might be followed along a different path. There is something of the lively independent tradition in psychoanalysis that runs through the ideas here.

The challenge for the therapist is to permit a measured suspension of familiar formalities in order for the patient to unfold their imaginings, metaphors, and visualizations in the potential space of the therapy room—the "as-if-ness" of transferential encounter where previous patterns of relating can be brought alive in the here and now. The idea of a freed dramatic encounter gives light to the way in which Freud's idea of free association can be applied. Pedder does not offer an account of how the physical environment should be established to create the most conducive conditions for interaction, that is to say, how the room should look, should there be artefacts, and so on. Although, there is no account of artistic material (paints, clay, etc.); instead, the space is presented as a mental space of creative encounter. Pedder is careful to deal with the situation where reality can collapse into unreality for some clients, in the case of psychosis, for instance, where the sense of as-if-ness might be lost. He offers several exemplars, from the child who loses a sense of reality about the pretend *Peter Pan* game with the crocodile, to an anecdote about seeing a play where the actors were in the audience, conflating the distance between audience and actor in a way which was unexpected and challenging. These experiences are used to demonstrate the way in which the margins between playing and reality can sometimes be fused. With further examples from literature and drama (Pirandello, Burnett, Carroll, Shakespeare), Pedder does not stoop to provide guidelines on how the therapist manages clinical situations; instead, he leaves the space for us to reflect on how we and our clients might experience, or have experienced, such situations ourselves.

There are several points of debate here: for instance, Pedder's assertion that all art is illusion. Pedder's point is, to be fair, rather about art appreciation than about how an artefact might vitalize or revitalize an experience in the viewer. Like Socrates, Pedder seems to suggest that there is, after all, nothing new, and this does seem rather to inhibit the notion that art can synthesize experiences into new realities. Notwithstanding these points of debate, the chapter offers an inspiring reclamation of a more fluid role for play in the process of therapy with clients. It is in the encounter of creative energies, where the medical model of the clinical surgical theatre is superseded by the dramatic theatre of the mind, that the client can experience new ways of being.

References

McDougall, J. (1985). *Theatres of the Mind: Illusion and Truth on the Psychoanalytic Stage*. New York: Basic Books.

Miller, A. (1987). *The Drama of Being a Child: The Search for the True Self*. London: Virago.

The role of space and location in psychotherapy, play, and theatre

> "When I was a child, I spake as a child, I understood as a child, I thought as a child: but when I became a man, I put away childish things. For now we see through a glass, darkly; but then face to face . . .
>
> (1 Corinthians 13:11, 12)

This paper explores common links between psychotherapy, play, and theatre, especially where they take place and what conditions are necessary to bring them to life, so that we can see through the glass less darkly. Trainee therapists beginning psychotherapy either individually or in a group ask, "Do we begin the session, or do we leave it to the patients and remain silent?; should we look at patients or avoid their gaze either in individual therapy or in a group when singled out for a communication at the beginning?" The question of technique here is, "What is the right level of tension needed to set psychotherapy going".

Prominent among my various starting points was the work of Winnicott that developed out of his original paper, "transitional objects and transitional phenomena" (1953), leading to the series of studies assembled in his book *Playing and Reality* (Winnicott, 1971). A further starting point for me arose from reflecting on the increased skill needed by actors in the modern theatre when they are not sheltered or framed by the traditional proscenium arch, with its obvious parallel problem for the therapist when not sheltered by traditional medical frames of reference such as uniforms or institutions. This discussion of psychotherapy is initially tallied to what is variously known as dynamic, analytically orientated, interpretative, or insight-orientated psychotherapy. However, the concept of insight is fraught with difficulties, as pointed out by Aubrey Lewis (1934). Here, the older meaning he gives is relevant: "originally it meant internal sight, that is to say, seeing with the eyes of the mind, having inner vision and discernment". Yet, how can we see into other people's minds? As Hayman (1974) said, "Unlike the sciences—the humanities, history and many other disciplines—what we constantly discuss are things that we literally cannot see or visualize". That is why some feel more comfortable with a presentation of repertory grids where an attempt is made to present a patient's inner world in pictorial terms that we can all see and measure. As a surgical colleague once said, "Surgery is so satisfying because you can look and see if your diagnosis is right."

The word "theatre" has intersecting origins—a place for looking—and so it came to be used in the "anatomy theatre" with its tiers for spectators and, hence, also in the "operating theatre". Two assumptions are made about psychotherapy and theatre: in dynamic psychotherapy, the essential task of the therapist is to help his patient get in touch with those aspects of his inner psychic world which have hitherto been denied, suppressed, or disowned. The task of the theatrical director is to help his actors bring to life the creation of the inner psychic world of the dramatist, as it is revealed through his characters in the play. Until psychotherapy begins, the inner world of the patient may remain largely hidden and unconscious until it is brought to life in the play of psychotherapy. Until rehearsals of a play begin, the inner world of the dramatist remains hidden in the script and out of public consciousness until brought to life on stage. During rehearsals, the producer encourages his players to mine within themselves to discover feeling states which resonate with those intended by the author's inner world; during psychotherapy the therapist's task is to help the patient mine within his own inner world.

Both therapist and director must create and facilitate the conditions necessary for this to occur: another expression of Winnicott's (1965) comes obviously to mind; the "facilitating environment". The question to be pursued is: what is the "location" of psychotherapy and theatre and what are the best facilitating conditions to foster each? What sort of space do we need, in which something can be brought to life for us to see? Clearly, there is another overlap here, with the whole subject of children's play, on which Winnicott (1971) has written so illuminatingly. "Play", he writes, "is neither a matter of inner psychic reality nor a matter of external reality"; "if play is neither inside nor outside, where is it?" (*ibid.*, p. 96). His answer is that it takes place in an interpsychic encounter, a "potential space between the individual and the environment, that which initially both joins and separates the baby and the mother" (*ibid.*, p. 103). In other words, play is no longer a mere daydream or fantasy, nor yet real in the everyday sense, but something in-between: inner world imaginings brought to life in the space between the child and his environment.

Winnicott (1971) writes similarly of psychotherapy:

> Psychotherapy takes place in the overlap of two areas of playing, that of the patient and that of the therapist. Psychotherapy has to do with two people playing together. The corollary of this is that where playing is not possible then the work done by the therapist is directed towards bringing the patient from a state of not being able to play into a state of being able to play. [*ibid.*, p. 38]

In other words, what has hitherto been more or less denied as inner fantasy is brought to life in the space between patient and therapist. It is suggested that in the theatre, too, the inner fantasy of the dramatist is brought to life in the potential space between the author and the audience, the space which the actors inhabit. Winnicott (1953) originally used "the terms 'transitional objects' and 'transitional phenomena' for designation of the intermediate area of experience, between the thumb and the teddy bear, between oral eroticism and the true object-relationship" that was imagined (mouth and mother). He repeatedly asked for the paradox of the transitional object to be respected. We must never ask, "did you conceive of this or was it presented to you from without?" (p. 12). We are in the field of illusion. "Gradual disillusionment" (p. 13) is one of the normal tasks of growing up in which a baby needs mother's help. Normally healthy people must undergo the same process of disillusionment each morning on waking from a dream. I can remember the day I sadly realized as a child that the coals in the fire were not fiery castles with magic caves between, but mere coals. Yet the capacity to return to the enjoyment of such illusions is essential for the appreciation of all forms of art.

We know that the actors in a play are real people, yet we believe in them as the characters they portray. We suspend disbelief. We tolerate the paradox. Good theatre depends on it. If the actors cannot make us believe in the part they are playing, the drama does not work. On the other hand, when we have no means of checking on the reality of the actors (for example, in radio productions) we may be more than convinced, or even deluded, about the reality of the fiction. This happens in a mundane way when people send presents to the characters in a radio serial, such as *The Archers* (BBC Radio 4), or, more alarmingly, when people believed that the radio broadcast of H. G. Wells' story *War of the Worlds* was for real. The same paradox is apparent in a child's game. A child knows you are both Daddy and the crocodile chasing him (in *Peter Pan*, of course, the crocodile eats the bad Daddy, Captain Hook, of the dream and becomes both). But a small, two- or three-year-old may suddenly become overwhelmed by the reality of the play and fear being eaten, so real Daddy must re-emerge quickly. This again is a question of the right level of tension. As Winnicott (1971, p. 52) says, "playing is inherently exciting and precarious" but "the pleasurable element in playing carries with it the implication that the instinctual arousal is not excessive".

Again, in formal psychotherapy, the paradox is needed. In analytic psychotherapy (individual or group), one sets up a relationship or working alliance (Greenson, 1965) between the therapist and the healthy adult part of the patient to investigate the way in which this relationship is distorted by the less mature child part of the patient; the distortion of the relationship we call transference, or the way in which our current perception of people in relationships is distorted by residues of feelings about important people in the past, and in particular parents. Pontalis (1974) refers to the "private theatre" of transference. Interpretative analytic psychotherapy can only work when the patient has sufficient capacity or ego strength to recognize and tolerate the paradox that though he may have intense feelings towards the therapist "as if" he were a parent, yet in reality he is not. In Winnicott's (1971) words, "psychotherapy is done in the overlap of the two play areas, that of the patient and that of the therapist" (p. 54). When the "as if" quality is lost, we say the transference has become psychotic.

Anna Freud (1936) was possibly getting at the same idea when she wrote,

> The ego is, in fact, requested to be silent and the id is invited to speak and promised that its derivatives shall not encounter the usual difficulties if they emerge into consciousness. Thus we have to play a double game with the patient's instinctual impulses, on the one hand encouraging them to express themselves and, on the other, steadily refusing them gratification—a procedure which incidentally gives rise to one of the numerous difficulties in the handing of analytic technique. [p. 12]

Freud is often quoted as saying that psychoanalysis was impossible with psychotic patients because no transference developed. This view derives from his theory of narcissism (Freud, 1914c), according to which psychotic patients had withdrawn all libido from external objects and redirected it towards their own ego; therefore, it appeared to follow that there was no libido available for the outgoing development of transference feelings towards the therapist. However, rather than no transference developing, the problem with the process of psychotherapy of people suffering psychosis is that the therapist may be drowned in the transference and that there may be insufficient ego available in the patient to take a look at the delusional distortions occurring. What Milner (1971) has referred to in the arts as the "conscious acceptance of the as-if-ness" is lost.

The appreciation of metaphor again depends on the acceptance and toleration of a paradox. Note that the word "metaphor" is really the Greek for "transference" (Dr John Padel, personal communication), literally both mean a "carrying across"—in this case of meaning from one area to another. If we say, "Mr X is a fox", most of us understand the implication that he is a sly fellow; the psychotic might take the allusion more concretely, as with the interpretation of proverbs. A capacity to think in metaphor is essential in both therapist and patient for picking up oblique allusions in psychotherapy. A patient whose tense and stubborn silences had yielded little for some while to classical interpretations about sphincter control and her fears of making a mess, suddenly sees the point when (providing her own metaphor) she laughs and says that the caretaker of her flats is always asking if she has been away because there is never any rubbish in her dustbin.

Another patient, whose fees had remained constant for some time and not been mentioned, says that she has just renewed her rail season ticket and feels very guilty that the clerk forgot to charge her the new increase which was due. Of course, she was also (metaphorically) referring to her guilt in the transference over the fees, which could then be brought into the open and discussed. As Wright (1976) puts it in a recent paper, "Metaphor and symptom":

> 1: Both symbolic structures (metaphor and symptom) present one thing in the semblance of another; but whereas the symptom conceals and leads to a restriction of view, metaphor reveals and leads out towards new vision. 2: the symptom is a wordless presentation of an unnameable dilemma—an abortive metaphor that stops below the level of speech. . . . 3: the undoing of a symptom is in part the creation of a metaphor from symptom. "Where id was there ego shall be". Where symptom was there metaphor shall be.

All these points were well illustrated by a patient seen in consultation, who initially had gone to her GP complaining that she was disgusted with her nose. The GP responded concretely to her symptom and referred her to a plastic surgeon, who, thinking there was little abnormal about her nose, referred her on. Her opening words were most impressive, in the sense that psychic change had already begun. She said, "When I first went to my doctor, I thought I was disgusted with my nose; now I'm beginning to see I'm really disgusted with myself and particularly my sexual feelings because I'm a lesbian." Leaving aside questions such as the displacement upwards of a concern about the genitalia to a concern about the face, she had already herself begun to replace symptom with metaphor, so that it was possible for her to see further into her problem. "New vision" had been opened up. Hayman (1974), too, points out how we use metaphors to conjure up a picture of what is not visualizable and how the capacity to visualize plays an essential part in the whole development and experience of conceptual thinking, which is grossly interfered with in children born blind. This particular problem is discussed by Langer (1942) who refers to the "dawn of language" upon the mind of Helen Keller, when her teacher passed her hand under the spout of a well and spelled into the other the word "water".

To return to the central theme: the creation of the right level of tension (or anxiety) for the paradox to emerge and be sustained. We all know from the Yerkes–Dodson Law that there is an optimum level of anxiety for the performance of a task. Too much anxiety and psychotherapy is impossible; too little and the dialogue remains chit-chat and the creative play never gets off the ground. Again, we are reminded of Winnicott's statement that playing is pleasurable if "the instinctual arousal is not excessive". My first experience of live theatre as a child was of traditional Christmas pantomime in a large Hippodrome with a proscenium arch stage. It would have been silly to ask where the drama took place. We obviously sat in the real world, but across the footlights the princes, princesses, fairies, and flying dancers occupied a magic world. Disbelief was totally suspended; they were clearly no mortals. This view of the theatre confirms in a concrete way the original meaning of the word "theatre" as a place where we look. We look through the proscenium arch to the stage where the drama occurs. Actors and audience are quite separate—a place where we can look, as in the medieval anatomy theatre, at people performing distinct roles in distinct costumes. Contrast this with a visit to a contemporary fringe theatre club, where the action may take place in and among the tables. Where is the drama now? We look at the actors. They have to be even more careful to follow the normal dramatic convention of not looking at us. If we exchanged glances it would confirm our relationship as real people. They avoid this reality contact so that the play can come alive in the space between us. Similarly, children absorbed in a game can be watched, but often prefer to remain unseen: "don't see me"—or the suspension of disbelief in their play collapses. It would be very cruel to say to a child clutching its transitional object, "That's only a rag".

There is a parallel about looking in psychotherapy. In classical psychoanalysis the patient, lying on a couch, unable to see the analyst, creates the optimum conditions for the activation of fantasy material and feelings about the analyst, which may be considerable distortions of reality. At the same time, many analysts observe the normal courteous convention of looking directly at the patient at the beginning and end of the session. As well as being part of normal civilized behaviour, this helps to anchor some patients back in the world of reality. By contrast, if psychotherapy is conducted absolutely face to face, there is far less space for the play of psychotherapy to develop in. Sometimes, this suppressive effect on fantasy may be desired, for example, with a borderline or psychotic patient. In group psychotherapy there is a similar problem: patients may try to single out a therapist for a direct "one-on-one" talk. It is sometimes helpful to avoid the direct gaze of the patient trying to do this, and focus instead on the centre of the group space, the aim being to get in touch with the fantasies of the group members about each other and the therapist and to suspend for a while more reality-based adult feelings.

To return to the theatre; I saw *Equus* (Shaffer, 1973) at the National Theatre from the few tiers of seats at the back of the stage: a complete reversal of the normal viewpoint. Unknown to us as we entered, some of the actors were already seated in the front row of these seats—in contemporary dress and, therefore, undistinguished from the true audience (rather as one might look in through a two-way screen and be unable at first to distinguish patients and therapists in a group). As the house lights dimmed, the opening actors left their seats and took their places in the space between the two audiences, and, with a most impressive power and control, began to bring the play to life before us, emphasizing that drama occurs not in a fixed place, but in a space between people.

"Playing implies trust" (Winnicott, 1971, p. 51); so does the theatre. We assume the revolver is loaded with blanks and not bullets. The corollary is that providing the space needed for psychotherapy, play, or theatre has to be the responsibility of a trustworthy figure. As therapist, parent, play-group leader, or stage manager, we have to see that there is a safe space into which there will be a minimum of unjustifiable intrusion. As Winnicott says (*ibid.*, p. 50), "responsible persons must be available when children play", not to organize overmuch, but to provide and protect the space. We must also provide proper play space for all children. It is interesting how the expression "play groups" has come into our language to express the need felt for the under-fives as a desirable preliminary to proper intellectual growth and functioning during later education. Wright (1976) is getting at the same idea when he says, "the analyst offers himself as the guardian of a potential space in which meaning may arise", "he takes over the facilitating function of the parent in its dual aspect and protects a developmental space against its premature closure".

This recalls Balint's (1957) warnings against premature responses to the patient's offers of symptoms. The GP who sent the girl disgusted with her nose straight off to a plastic surgeon well illustrated this. Michael and Enid Balint (1961) have described the function of the doctor in educating a patient about his illness, which they feel has earned doctors their courtesy title, as:

> that aspect of the doctor's teaching function which may be called the shaping of the patient's illness. This happens by an interaction that has been described elsewhere as the "patient's offers" of illnesses and "the doctor's responses" to them. Using a simile from gardening, one could say that the patient grows an illness and it is the doctor who trains it by pruning some symptoms, allowing others to go on growing, while forcing yet others to take a direction that he prescribes to them. Of course, the doctor cannot do everything, his powers are as limited as the gardener's. [p. 105]

A children's story that some might now consider dated and sentimental, but which has delighted generations, is *The Secret Garden* by Burnett (1911). It unites three themes I have attempted to show the links between: it is not only drama, but is also about the value of play, and, most of all, a tale of a successful therapy for all concerned. Mary is orphaned as a little girl in India and is sent home to the care of her uncle, an embittered recluse in a vast, rambling house in the middle of the Yorkshire moors. Slowly, she discovers that also in this house lives Colin, a crippled child, hidden away on a sick-bed. It is prophesied that Colin will not live and his father (Mary's uncle) cannot bear to see Colin, who reminds him of the fact that the child's mother (his adored wife) died at his birth. The mother had particularly enjoyed a walled garden within the larger gardens, but since her death the key has been lost and no one is allowed to talk of the garden, let alone enter it. Needless to say, Mary finds the key and sets about restoring the garden with the help of Dickon, a boy of the moors, a Pan or id personified, who intimately understands the ways of animals and plants. Up until now, Colin's tantrums, outbursts, and self-pity have been too much for the domestic staff allotted to care for him and they have colluded with his (and his father's) illness and its manipulations. Mary will have none of this; she arranges for Colin to be brought secretly to the walled garden. With the aid of Dickon and his magic in making things grow, Colin slowly learns to walk, to live, and is restored to full health, which in turn cures father's grief and melancholy.

A sentimental tale perhaps, whose ending is predictable from the beginning. Yet, it illustrates one of my main themes: that a space is needed—a secret garden in which life can grow. Mary found the key to it. I often think psychotherapy is like gardening—you provide the soil and do a bit of pruning (as Balint has said) but the growth has to come from the plant/patient. A rather borderline patient sent me a pot-plant at Christmas, after she had stopped coming, with a label which read: "Because you helped make me grow".

Exploration of the concept of space runs throughout the writings of Masud Khan. In a fascinating essay on "Montaigne, Rousseau and Freud", Khan (1970) proposes the idea that self exploration via "crucial friendship with the other became exigent only when there was a gap left by the absence of God's presence; and the first example of this is Montaigne's relation to La Boétie in the sixteenth century". After La Boétie's death, Montaigne established a private space in his library at Château de Montaigne for himself, and in this space he lived through an extremely devout relationship to an inner presence, which was not that of God, but that of another human being.

This echoes Winnicott's (1958) view that "the capacity to be alone is based on the experience of being alone in the presence of someone [i.e. originally Mother], and that without a sufficiency of this experience the capacity to be alone cannot develop" (p. 33). Montaigne was alone in his library in the internal presence of La Boétie.

Khan (1971, 1972a) explores further the concept of therapeutic space and points out that child analysts in particular (for example, Winnicott with his "Squiggle Game") have contributed much to enlarging the scope of the analytic space. Khan (1977) tells the story of a female patient who (at the age of three and a half years), following the traumatic changes associated with the birth of younger twins, had buried in the garden a pair of the family's silver candlesticks. She kept the secret of the loss from them for six years. Khan felt this secret, which was re-enacted in the analytic setting, to have been an important potential space in which the patient had been able to keep alive some part of herself that she could later contact again, as Colin does in the secret garden.

A patient of mine in analysis used to be an art student, but gave up her painting completely when she got married and had children. Her husband had left her, the children were leaving home, and she had been profoundly depressed. For some time, she never mentioned a portfolio of her old paintings and drawings which she had hidden away rather uncaringly in the garage. She had once nearly thrown them away, and her husband had taken responsibility for preserving them. She brought me this portfolio to look at and wanted me to preserve it for her. It seemed to represent a part of herself that she had lost and sought to re-contact within the potential space of the analytic consulting room. Foulkes (1964) mentions, among several influences that developed his thinking in the 1930s, Pirandello's (1921) play *Six Characters in Search of an Author*, and Abse (1974) enlarges on this. In the play, a director is considering a new production of a Pirandello play when six players arrive, "declaring that they are characters abandoned by a playwright". Against the director's initial protests, they enact their own drama.

> The dramatist in this case was, of course, really Luigi Pirandello. ... It is the externalized drama of a rejected inner drama. Had the characters been accepted by his imagination their drama would have been organized altogether differently. [Abse, 1974, pp. 100–101]

We are constantly invited to consider and are confused as to what is illusion and what reality. Pirandello himself felt he had no life outside his writing; it was presumably locked in his inner world.

He wrote in his journal, "There is someone who is living my life. And I know nothing about him".

Pirandello's split-off inner world reappears in the play, just as a patient's split-off inner world might, during the course of psychotherapy, reappear in a dream, or a child's in play therapy. This conflict between the inner world and reality is illustrated by an early exchange between the Producer and one of the characters (Father):

PRODUCER: But what do you want here?

FATHER: We wish to live, sir!

PRODUCER: Through all eternity?

FATHER: No, sir; just for a moment . . . in you. . . .

PRODUCER: And where's the script?

FATHER: It is in us, sir. The drama is in us. We are the drama and we are impatient to act it—so fiercely does our inner passion urge us on.

Father's plea, "We wish to live . . . just for a moment in you" seems to express the cry of the child or lost self part of the patient seeking a potential space for growth. The theme of a play within a play is, of course, a common device in drama; just as the dream within a story is in literature. The latter is an essential element of some of the best known children's stories, for example, Carroll's *Alice in Wonderland*, with its schizophreniform dream, Barrie's *Peter Pan*, in which the children fly away as if in a dream at night, and Milne's dramatized version of *The Wind in the Willows*. And the same themes present themselves in Shakespeare's *Hamlet*. The familiar psychoanalytic view of *Hamlet* as a variant of an Oedipal theme was first suggested by Freud (1900a) in a footnote and expanded by Ernest Jones (1910). As Freud puts it (p. 264, fn.):

the changed treatment of the same material reveals the whole difference in the mental life of these two widely separated epochs of civilization: the secular advance of repression in the emotional life of mankind. In the Oedipus the child's wishful fantasy that underlies it is brought into the open and realized as it would be in a dream. In Hamlet it remains repressed; and, just as in the case of a neurosis, we only learn of its existence from its inhibiting consequences.

Oedipus unknowingly killed his father, became King, and married his mother. Hamlet, knowing his father is dead, fails either to become King or to marry his mother; but his uncle succeeds in both, having himself killed the King.

Almost exactly this had happened to a young man in psychotherapy who suffered an acute obsessional breakdown with fears of harming others with knives. His father had died suddenly in the night. This mobilized all his guilt over old Oedipal wishes and he feared he might have got up at night and stabbed his father, so that he was greatly relieved at the inquest to hear the pathologist's report that there were no marks of violence on the body and death was from myocardial infarction. He then lived alone with his mother and all went well for a while until his mother remarried his uncle, when he began to fear he might get up at night and stab him, so began locking up the knives at night and finally broke down. To return to Hamlet: Knights (1974) writes of the "increasing inwardness" of Shakespeare's plays: "As the plays succeed one another . . . the action . . . is used to project an inner truth in which each one of us finds some aspect or potentiality of himself"; "One way of putting it might be to say that the plays move closer to the dream, in which the dreamer is all the characters". If we accept this view that the characters in Shakespeare's tragedies can be seen as aspects of his and our own inner world, what then? The details of the historical Hamlet provide a peg for the exploration of Hamlet's and, thus, Shakespeare's own inner world, which finds resonance in each one of us. Hamlet's Oedipal wish, that his father should die, has come true. Hamlet's guilt is suggested by the appearance of the Ghost/hallucination demanding vengeance and by his acute suicidal depression:

> O, that this too too sullied flesh would melt,
> Thaw and resolve itself into a dew,
> Or that the Everlasting had not fixed
> His canon 'gainst self-slaughter. O God, God,
> How weary, stale, flat, and unprofitable
> Seem to me all the uses of this world!
> Fie on't, ah fie, 'tis an unweeded garden [I.ii. 129]

Yet, his guilt is not consciously acknowledged, for it is split off and projected into his image of his uncle, whose conjugal acts with mother he can then deplore. "To post with such dexterity to incestuous sheets" (I.ii. 157). As Jones (1949, p. 88) says, "In reality his uncle incorporates the deepest and most buried part of his own personality so that he cannot kill him without also killing himself", which is, of course, what ultimately happens. Now to the play within the play. Cries Hamlet, "The play's the thing / Wherein I'll catch the conscience of the king" (II.ii. 608). Who is the King, but a split-off aspect of Hamlet himself; so, is he really saying that the play within the play, like a dream, will reveal his own unconscious guilt?

> I have heard
> That guilty creatures sitting at a play
> Have by the very cunning of the scene
> Been struck so to the soul that presently
> They have proclaimed their malefactions [II.ii. 592]

The King also paradoxically appears to understand more of Hamlet than he does himself when he says (of Hamlet): "What it should be, / More than his father's death, that thus hath put him / So much from th'understanding of himself, / I cannot dream of" (II.ii. 7). And later: "There's something in his soul / O'er which his melancholy sits on brood (III.i. 167). Taken at their face value, neither of these remarks make any sense, as the King knows perfectly well what is troubling Hamlet. Freud's (1912e) original idea of the analyst as the well-polished mirror reflecting back the patient to himself is well known, though nowadays it can seem rather too cold and unyielding a metaphor. The idea of the mirror is twice used by Hamlet; once when Hamlet (and, therefore, Shakespeare) advised the players on acting: "the purpose of playing, whose end, both at the first, and now, was and is, to hold as 'twere, the mirror up to nature" (III.ii. 20), and, second, when he goes to his mother's apartment (with Polonius behind the arras) and says to her: "You shall not budge, / You go not till I set you up a glass / Where you may see the inmost part of you" (III.iv. 18).

Winnicott (1967a) explored the idea that the infant's self image is built up through seeing himself reflected in his mother's face.

This glimpse of the baby's and child's seeing the self in the mother's face, and afterwards in a mirror, gives a way of looking at analysis and at the psychotherapeutic task. Psychotherapy is not making clever and apt interpretations; by and large, it is giving the patient back what the patient brings. The therapist (like the actor or artist) has to set up a glass and hold it long enough to facilitate "the acceptance of both illusion and disillusion" (Milner, 1971). "Gradual disillusionment" is a necessary part of every infant's development. A similar process of disillusionment happens to all of us on waking from a dream, or to the patient recovering from the nightmare of a psychotic breakdown. It is an essential part of the ending of any successful psychoanalytic therapy when the patient comes to be disillusioned about the threatening power of inner monsters or gross projections into the outer world, when inside and outside can be faced without the need for distortion. And, of course, it happens when the house lights go up at the end of a play. As Prospero says towards the end ot *The Tempest*,

> Our revels now are ended. These our actors,
> As I foretold you, were all spirits, and
> Are melted into air, into thin air;
> And, like the baseless fabric of this vision,
> The cloud-capped towers, the gorgeous palaces,
> The solemn temples, the great globe itself,
> Yea, all which it inherit, shall dissolve,
> And, like this insubstantial pageant faded,
> Leave not a rack behind: we are such stuff
> As dreams are made on; and our little life
> Is rounded with a sleep. [IV.i. 148]

Commentary (GW) on Chapter Two: Attachment and new beginnings

I n Chapter One, the anecdote about the blurring of the audience and the cast in a performance of *Equus* at the National Theatre brings to the fore the question of boundaries and the therapeutic space. In this chapter, Pedder revisits this in a more technical discussion of aspects of attachment in the process of therapy. He begins by building theory that links the work of Michael Balint with the better known research of John Bowlby. In particular, the similarities between Bowlby's work on problem "attachment patterns" and Balint's observations of "basic fault" and "clinging" are drawn. In connecting Balint and Bowlby, Pedder locates Bowlby along the trajectory of the "independent school" of psychoanalysis. Pedder marks his own point of departure from Freud's assertion that therapeutic relationships are keyed by erotic affiliation, because, in the end, Pedder favours Bowlby's formulations, based on the bonds of attachment, where love, security, and anxiety are more prominent than the Freudian erotic. The rub of the debate oscillates around a case account which highlights how disruption of attachment during childhood can be manifest in depression in adult life. In this case study, Pedder demonstrates how therapy offers a reparative synthesis and a new attachment.

One of the most intriguing parts of this case is how Pedder manages the patient's requests for him to hold her hand. We see the careful thought that goes into his withholding at first and then his decision to break with standard analytic Freudian protocol of "abstinence" and submit to her request. Pedder examines the controversial question of the use of touch in psychoanalytic therapy and, in precise detail, rejuvenates Ferenczi's ideas about "active technique". Pedder tells us he agrees with Balint that to touch a patient's hand during analysis is not necessarily a counter therapeutic act and, with much forethought, an event like touching a patient's hand may yield therapeutic gain. The fine grain in this case where Pedder is confronted with the touch dilemma is illustrated with painstaking detail. While other therapeutic denominations would not give a second thought to such a request, Pedder's caution exemplifies his attention to micro-dynamics in the therapeutic procedure. Even if one favours the non-touch rule as a matter of course, it is still worth considering the alternative position.

We are made aware in this chapter of Pedder's own generational lineage as one of the best known exponents of the independent tradition of psychoanalysis. The independent school was set apart from the Kleinians and the Freudians, and its ancestry can be seen to run a course from the Hungarian Sandor Ferenczi through to Michael Balint and beyond. Ferenczi, initially a close adherent of Freud, was the first to adopt a much more fluid and active approach to the psychoanalytic method. Freud (1913c) admitted that the cold texture of instantiating the resistance as a rationale for using the couch, whereby the patient would lie back with the analyst out of sight behind, was not a technique endorsed by all his colleagues. Ferenczi (1929) believed relaxation, not resistance, was prescient in advancing the therapeutic situation, where the authoritarian re-enactment of the physician–patient or teacher–pupil situation was superseded by a more equalized and familiar engagement between therapist and patient. Ferenczi (1929) developed what became known as the "active technique", whereby he would permit his patients to move about freely and locate themselves in the consulting space wherever they felt comfortable. He admitted that this was a shift away from Freud:

> In the course of my practical analytical work, which extended over many years, I constantly found myself infringing one or another of

Freud's injunctions in his *Recommendations on Technique*. For instance, my attempt to adhere to the principle that patients must be in a lying position during analysis would at times be thwarted by their uncontrollable impulse to get up and walk about the room or speak to me face to face. [*ibid.*, p. 110]

We can see Klein's development of her play technique in relation to Ferenczi's influence on her as her second analyst, after Karl Abraham. However, Ferenczi's own active technique has been consigned to a place of relative chagrin in the history of the psychoanalytic movement. Yet, we see here Pedder tentatively rescuing Ferenczi, in this case "hand holding", as an infringement of both medical and psychotherapeutic orthodoxy. I think rather than see this as radical modification of technique, it is correct to locate Pedder's work along the continuum of his own vision of an active, flexible and engaging form of psychoanalytic therapy.

References

Ferenczi, S. (1929). The principle of relaxation and neocatharsis. In: *Final Contributions to Psychoanalysis* (pp. 108–125). London: Hogarth, 1955.

Freud, S. (1913c). On beginning the treatment. *S.E.*, *12*: 121–144. London: Hogarth.

Attachment and new beginnings

Background

I n Balint's writings on regression and primary object love (1937, 1952, 1968) he frequently speaks of "an instinct to cling". This comes close to Bowlby's view (1958, 1969, 1973, 1975) on the instinctual basis of attachment behaviour. Bowlby's definitive three-volume work (1969, 1973, 1980) crowns a lifetime's researches into the early and late effects of childhood separation. He has recently summarized this work (Bowlby, 1975). In his reconsideration of instinct theory he argues that attachment behaviour should be "conceived as a class of behaviour that is distinct from feeding behaviour and sexual behaviour and of at least as equal significance in human life". He considers the most likely function of attachment behaviour is protection, mainly from predators, and therefore crucial to the survival of the species.

Bowlby's work has been criticized (e.g., Engel, 1971) for discarding the dynamic and economic points of view and not adequately distinguishing psychological from behavioural frames of reference. However, as Matte-Blanco (1971) more favourably comments, its impact upon ideas regarding the psychobiological foundations of psychoanalysis is bound to be great. It is suggested here that Bowlby's concept of attachment behaviour could provide the psychobiological foundation which Balint was looking for.

Balint (1968) twice speaks of "attachment behaviour": once (p. 169) in discussing the "ocnophilic bias of our modern technique" when he refers to "object-seeking, clinging, attachment behaviour", and earlier (p. 165), in referring to Bowlby (1958), when he noted that these phenomena had been known for some considerable time and more recently under the influence of ethology as "attachment behaviour".

This paper pursues these links and also discusses, in the light of Bowlby's view of the importance of attachment behaviour, the question of whether it can ever be appropriate to gratify a patient's wish for physical contact with the analyst, for example, the wish to hold a hand, during a period of regression in analysis. Balint (1968) makes a valuable distinction between malignant "regression aimed at gratification" and more benign "regression aimed at recognition". The former might occur in hysterical patients whose problems lie in the area of Oedipal conflict and belongs to three-person psychology. Few would suggest that the regressive wishes of such patients should be gratified. We accept Freud's (1915a, p. 165) dictum, "The treatment must be carried out in abstinence". Language and interpretation should suffice, though, interestingly enough, Freud himself soon modified this to, "Analytic treatment should be carried through as far as is possible, under privation—in a state of abstinence" (Freud, 1919g, p. 162). The more benign regression may occur in those whose problem lies at the level of what Balint has termed the "basic fault" and belongs to two-person psychology. In the latter type of case, the regression may herald a "new beginning" if the patient's needs are recognized and met. Khan (1969) makes the distinction between these two levels very clear in his essay on Balint's researches on the theory of psychoanalytic technique. At the area of the Oedipal level, "the provision of frustrations" is the key; in the area of the basic fault "the provision of recognitions" may be essential to a new beginning.

Balint first mentioned such needs in 1937: "Very often these wishes do not go further than to be able to touch the analyst, to cling to him, or to be touched or stroked by him". Yet, he provided few details of how he actually met such needs. Thus, he writes

(1968, p. 133), "Another patient . . . wanted and had to hold one of my fingers for quite some time during a particular period of her analysis". A little later, he refers to "some sort of physical contact with the analyst, the most frequent form of which is the holding of the analyst's hand, or one of his fingers, or touching his chair". Yet, Balint does not seem quite sure how to understand such needs in terms of instinct theory. Of the first example he writes, "with a little effort one could find—or create—an instinct to cling for the explanation of the satisfaction observed in her case" (p. 134), whereas further on he says "this contact is definitely libidinous and on occasions may even be highly charged" (p. 145).

Now, "an instinct to cling", which Balint had first mentioned in his 1937 paper, sounds very like the expression of attachment behaviour, whereas, if the "contact is definitely libidinous", this sounds more like the gratification of an erotic instinct, which so alarms us all because of Freud's original reservations and the consequences of Ferenczi's "Grand Experiments". Balint has reviewed the tragic disagreement between Freud and Ferenczi in this area (1968, p. 149–156), which he feels made it so hard for he himself (Balint) to get the subject a fair hearing. Although Balint can speak of an "instinct to cling", it seems hard for him not to think of it as something erotic. When he writes (1952, p. 231), "the level of gratification never goes beyond that of mild fore-pleasure", this seems to be subsuming hand-holding under the heading of erotic behaviour, as, of course, it could well be, whereas if we see hand-holding as at times an expression of attachment behaviour, our perspective shifts.

Bowlby (1958), in his review of the psychoanalytic literature on the nature of the child's tie to his mother, expresses the view that the Hungarian school comes closest to his ideas on attachment, and particularly in Balint's concept of primary object love. He quotes Balint (1937): "This form of object relationship is not linked to any of the erotogenic zones; it is not oral, oral-sucking, anal, genital, etc, love but is something on its own . . .". Winnicott (1960) appears to be making a similar distinction between meeting needs and satisfying instincts when he writes, "It must be emphasised that in referring to the meeting of infant needs I am not referring to the satisfaction of instincts" (p. 141). The case described here is also a good example of how, when a False Self becomes organised in an individual who has a high intellectual potential, there is a very strong tendency for the mind to become the location of the False Self, and in this case there develops a dissociation between intellectual activity and psychosomatic existence.

In the case I describe, the patient's breakdown occurred while pursuing a postgraduate degree which represented the interests of her false self.

My clinical case also illustrates Winnicott's (1960) comment;

In analysis of a False Personality the fact must be recognised that the analyst can only talk to the False Self of the patient about the patient's True Self. It is as if a nurse brings a child, and at first the analyst discusses the child's problem, and the child is not directly contacted. Analysis does not start until the nurse has left the child with the analyst, and the child has become able to remain alone with the analyst and has started to play. [p. 151]

Case history

A young teacher in her mid-twenties was referred by a general psychiatrist sympathetic to analysis. She had previously been under treatment from psychiatrists of a different school, and received heavy doses of mixed antidepressant drugs as an inpatient. She told me she had become depressed at the age of twenty-one, while doing a postgraduate degree abroad. She had returned home, been admitted to hospital for several months, and thereafter stood the heavy doses of drugs for some eighteen months. She was longing to talk to someone and "break down the shell around herself", which the drugs had only increased. She had often said to her previous psychiatrists that there were a lot of things she wanted to talk about but they had replied in the vein: "Never mind about that, we'll wait till you feel better".

She was the second of three siblings; she had a brother three years older and a sister two years younger. At first, she gave an idealized picture of her childhood: she had enjoyed primary school and all went well until she moved to secondary school. Father was a lawyer and worked long hours. Mother cared for the family, but seemed to have been not really available emotionally to the children. At secondary school, my patient was often away with minor physical illnesses, some of which she admitted she faked. After leaving school, she did a first degree and then won a scholarship to do a doctorate abroad, where her depressive breakdown occurred.

Towards the end of our first meeting she said she wanted "therapy" rather than "analysis", by which she meant something healing rather than dissecting, and we agreed to start with twice-weekly sessions. At our second meeting, she hesitated between the chair and the couch and then sat down. She thought I would expect her to use the couch; she needed to respond to others' expectations because she was afraid of revealing her real self. She felt she had lost her spontaneity at university; now she could only find herself secondhand, through literature. I suggested that this loss had perhaps happened much earlier in childhood and her early years had not been as ideal as she supposed. Her response to this in the next session was to tell me about her separation from her mother from eighteen months–two years, which had not emerged in the initial semi-formal history-taking. Mother had been ill during her next pregnancy and she had been sent to stay with an aunt for six months. She often feels that this aunt was more of a real mother, so the separation from her when she returned home at age two was even more painful. Thereafter, as a child, she was extremely anxious about further separations and very clinging if taken to a party. When they went on holiday she would always, as a priority, secretly locate the police station in case her parents should go away and leave her. At age ten this anxiety had (consciously) "switched off like a tap" to be replaced by the minor physical illnesses which often kept her away from secondary school.

With the history of childhood separation, I expected her to be anxious about holiday breaks and made prophylactic interpretations to that effect. However, she insisted at first that she was unaffected, and went away at school half-terms in addition to usual holidays. I had begun seeing her in January and, typically, at Easter, she denied she would miss me and arranged to go and look after a girlfriend abroad who was having emotional troubles. This "compulsive care taking" of others was a marked feature; she was at the time taking a special remedial class for backward and difficult children.

The treatment seemed to go well and she gradually weaned herself from all the drugs she had been on. We covered a lot of fairly obvious and classical analytic themes: for example, envy of her elder brother and his phallic capacities. She dreamt they went to a fairground shooting-range. He was given a good gun and she got one with a crooked barrel. Conversely, she was terrified of others' envy of her. At school, she hid her family's acquaintance with a well-known author and (during treatment) nearly hid from me that she had helped to make a television programme. In appearance she was a handsome girl with a fine head of hair, which, together with her dress, was in somewhat unisex style. The referring psychiatrist had mentioned sexual difficulties, but what she referred to as lesbian tendencies seemed so obviously like a search for the mother she had lost. Either she was interested in being cuddled and discovering whether her body was acceptable, or she related to women in a more narcissistic way and looked after them. She had a boyfriend throughout treatment, but someone who had been married, separated, not divorced, and had another girlfriend, so he was essentially unavailable, and this allowed her to remain uncommitted to either sex. She was determined not to acknowledge her needs at any level. Her sister she portrayed as the younger, pretty one who was prepared to seduce men to give her anything she wanted. "My sister makes up her mouth like a cunt", she once cried with indignation. She seemed determined to deny any needs of her own at oral or genital levels. She was especially afraid of revealing her needs to be loved and that if she said, "I need you" to a man, it might be mistaken for a sexual invitation.

Towards the summer break she was able to talk more of her feelings about the coming separation and how in her mother's presence she had sulked whenever depressed, but refused to let mother comfort her. She acknowledged her need for a companion on her journey of discovering herself (a *Sancho Panza*, she suggested) but feared I would be overwhelmed by her inner chaos. Just before the summer break she had a dream (prompted by seeing a girl she was attracted to in a shop) in which a chest of drawers (mother's breast) was snatched from her by her sister. We agreed that it related to the coming break and to childhood. She was afraid that men, or myself, or mother (who was always pressing her to get married) would take her away from women too soon. She did not read analytic works, but said spontaneously it was unfair that men do not have women's task of giving up their original sexual object choice. After the break, she reported a dream in which she did not bother to stop in her car to give mother a lift, thus reversing and revenging both the situation of the break and of the childhood separation.

In retrospect, I realize she perhaps had flu or colds and stayed away rather more than average—once obviously when she feared I was exasperated by her demands and she stayed in bed to nurse herself, thus repeating the pattern of adolescence. I think I missed these repetitions at the time because she was always so reasonable about ringing up to say she could not come. In October, she had a dream which seemed to herald the beginning of getting in touch with the child part of herself. She dreamt that a little girl was riding a tricycle (she knew she had been on tricyclic antidepressants), went head first into a brick wall and fell unconscious. Someone dialled 999, but when the ambulance arrived it was not needed because the little girl was beginning to recover consciousness. Just before the Christmas break, she overslept and missed a session in pre-emptive revenge. The next night she dreamt I was having a party for patients and she was excluded in a corner. Over Christmas, she had a homosexual affair, perhaps both in defiance of me and of mother (who is always pressing her to marry) and, at the same time, in search of mother.

And so we proceeded, gaining insights which interested her and seemed plausible, and yet there was still something missing. She had always resented the sexual stereotypes presented by her parents and copied by her older brother and younger sister. She defied both in a no-man's-land between the two. In June, she was rather more depressed when she seemed at last to be giving up her fantasy of a penis and arranged for the first time to see a gynaecologist herself about her dysmenorrhoea, as though beginning to accept her female identity. She protested, of course, at my commenting to this effect but seemed to confirm it by producing a dream in which she is given a pen that at first writes with yellow ink, but it then turns to blood.

After the second summer break, the child part of her appeared more in dreams and she seemed more in touch with the rage of this child when, for example, in a dream the child was being excluded by adults. And yet, there was very little sign of this protesting child during sessions. I had a growing sense of unease about this reasonableness and realized that I had probably colluded with her reasonable false-self organization because she was so agreeable and co-operative. I eventually made an intervention of unusual length for me, in which I told her of this feeling I had developed. I said I spoke with some hesitation because I did not want her to think I felt this co-operative part of her was at all phoney, superficial, or insincere; clearly it was a deep part of her character and had positive values, which made people depend and rely on her, though this in itself must be a problem for her because it made it even harder to reveal the unreasonable, protesting child-part of herself. Again, I said it was very agreeable the way she always came on time, marched straight to the couch, plonked herself down, and got straight on with her dreams and associations; the way she always rang to let me know if ill, and if my wife took the message she would say, "What a nice girl that sounds", etc., but that all this, charming and agreeable as it was, must be at considerable personal cost. Well, that did it. Of course, at the time she agreed with me as reasonably as ever, but three days later, after the weekend, she came rather earlier than usual and I found her in the waiting-room streaming with tears—certainly not put on just to show me another compliant aspect of herself, but dark, silent, painful depression. I arranged to see her daily when possible. She was terrified of her real self emerging and afraid of going mad. She felt "at the end of a springboard".

That week of black depression was followed the next Monday by hyperactivity and excitement. She had eaten and slept little over the weekend. She paced up and down the consulting room, smoking furiously. She sat in a hard chair, a soft chair, knelt or lay on the floor, or sat cross-legged, facing me, on the couch. She talked incessantly, at times incoherently. I nearly lost my nerve and thought of referring her back to the psychiatrist, fearing she might be a full-blown manic depressive after all, but managed to contain her excitement. She was clearly terrified of her "devouringness", which she was taking out on the cigarettes. She said that in letting herself see round my room she was "broadening her horizons" and, for the first time, daring to see the effect of herself on me. She had not considered this before, having had a fantasy of myself as the stage analyst writing notes behind her. On Wednesday of that week, we could not find a time to meet. She had a dream in two parts. In the first part there was a wounded elephant trapped in the corner of a cage; in the second part a friend (who, like herself, had been a refugee as a child) murdered a man. We agreed that the elephant was the child-part of her who had never forgotten how wounded she had felt over being a refugee, but that she was still terrified of the murderous rage she felt about it and about my not seeing her on Wednesday, which had to be put into the friend.

Her fear of her devouringness was intense. She even arranged to visit the dentist that week and she drank more than usual. Spontaneously, she reflected on the nature of remorse and of being "bitten back" for one's greed. Despite the distress of this period, she felt it to be a positive crisis and did not want to ease her distress with the drugs, which she still had available from before. She went home to her parents for the next weekend and felt able for the first time to get them to recognize her depression without her being in the least vindictive about it. Her next dream was of leading a sad orang-utang up to the back door of a nunnery, where they were left outside, peering in through the half-glass door (which is like my consulting room); clearly, the depressed, primitive part of herself, which she still feared, would be unacceptable to me. A few days later she dreamt she wanted Carol (the girlfriend to whom she was attracted) but Carol goes abroad (a reversal of the situation of her adult breakdown). She (the patient) has head lice in the dream. I said she feared I would reject her (like Carol) because of her lousy head. She turned over, face down, on the couch and buried her head in the pillow, extending her arms out loosely to either side of the pillow. Her hands moved around restlessly, reaching silently in my direction for some ten minutes. Eventually, I said I thought she wanted me to take her hand, though she felt unable to say so. And then I did. This seemed an important new beginning and she was later able to say that she had been terrified of being too demanding in asking me to hold a hand, fearing I might not trust her and might have mistaken her wish to be held as sexual.

About six weeks after the collapse of her false-self reasonableness she had a dream in three parts, which seemed to link up her whole life. Part 1: She was walking alone in a field looking for milk (as one might on holiday). In Part 2, she was a child with her mother and the aunt who had fostered her. They had arrived at a seaside resort (where she had, in fact, gone at age two, following the separation) looking for a boarding house. They had been promised a fine view of the sea, but, when shown around the boarding house, the windows were almost entirely bricked up and the sea was only just visible if you stood on the furniture. Mother could not afford anything better; she was too poor. In Part 3, she was an adult and went into a book shop, but the manager had nothing she wanted. It was like the library where her breakdown had occurred when she had felt so imprisoned by her books.

We agreed that the three parts linked up her whole life; her fear of being alone without milk/nourishment; her fear that I/mother would be too poor and not have the resources to offer her so that she would have to be boarded out with a poor view of the sea/ mother; and, third, her breakdown abroad where she had gone in compliance with her family's high academic standards and achievements, but had felt imprisoned in the books, as, indeed, she had also perhaps felt restricted in the earlier part of her treatment by the manager/myself who was not really then giving her what she wanted.

Discussion

Perhaps my experience with this case amounts to no more than a personal rediscovery of what many analysts have written about the two levels of analytic work and the insufficiency of work at a verbal level for some patients. Thus, Little (1960) writes, "Verbalisation then becomes the second stage in a two-stage process, both stages being necessary for real insight to be attained, but the second being only effective as a result of the first, i.e. of the body happening"; or Balint (1968, p. 134): "I wish to emphasise that the satisfaction did not replace interpretation, it was in addition to it. In some treatments interpretation preceded and in others followed satisfaction, as the situation demanded". Winnicott (1959) wrote,

> Only the true self can be analysed. Psychoanalysis of the false-self, analysis that is directed at what amounts to no more than an internalised environment, can only lead to disappointment. There may be an apparent early success. It is being recognised in the last few

years that in order to communicate with the true self where a false self has been given pathological importance it is necessary for the analyst first of all to provide conditions which will allow the patient to hand over to the analyst the burden of the internalised environment, and so to become a highly dependent but a real, immature, infant; then, and then only, the analyst may analyse the true self. This could be a present-day statement of Freud's anaclitic dependence in which the instinctual drive leans on the self-preservative. [p. 133]

And, perhaps, in place of this rather tortuous idea of one drive leaning on another, we could see anaclitic dependence as an expression of a single drive of attachment or an "instinct to cling". Khan (1972b) summarizes his view of the two levels thus:

It is my belief that in all psychotherapeutic work with patients, psychotherapists and analysts have to provide two distinct types of relating from their side. One type of relating is covered by interpretative work, which helps the patient to gain insight into his internal conflicts and thus resolve them. The other sort of relating, which is harder to define, is more in the nature of providing coverage for the patient's self-experience in the clinical situation. The knack of any psychotherapeutic work is to strike the right balance within these two types of functions in the therapist.

The anxiety about meeting the patient's needs at the deeper level seems to have been exaggerated by the fear of irreversible regression. Balint (1952, p. 231) saw no reason to modify what he had already written in 1937;

My clinical experience was briefly this: At times when the analytic work has already progressed a long way, i.e. towards the end of a cure, my patients began—very timidly at first—to desire, to expect, even to demand certain simple gratifications, mainly, though not exclusively, from their analyst. On the surface these wishes appeared unimportant: to give a present to the analyst or—more frequently—to receive one from him; to be allowed to touch or stroke him or to be touched or stroked by him, etc; and most frequently of all to be able to hold his hand or just one of his fingers. Two highly important characteristics of these wishes are easily seen. First: they can be satisfied only by another human being; any autocrotic satisfaction is simply impossible. Second: the level of gratification never goes beyond that of mild fore-pleasure. Correspondingly a really full satisfaction followed by an anticlimax can hardly ever be observed, only a more or less complete satura- tion. Thus, if satisfaction arrives at the right moment and with the right intensity, it leads to reactions which can be observed and recognised only with difficulty, as the level of pleasure amounts only to a tranquil quiet sense of well-being.

My patient demonstrated clearly both the need for "another human being" and the "tranquil quiet sense of well-being" after the need was met. She also confirmed that the "level of gratification never goes beyond that of a mild fore-pleasure" though, as empha- sized earlier, I feel that the very word "fore-pleasure" is here out of place, since the need that is being met is not really erotic, but the search for basic unity or attachment.

Commentary (GW) on Chapter Three: Failure to mourn and melancholia

P edder offers an account of the way in which psychoanalytic theory has progressed from the idea that "cathexis", or "libidinal withdrawal", is the basis of healthy mourning to the notion that internalization of the lost loved one is necessary to complete the task of mourning. Pedder tackles first Freud's main theoretical anchors in his theory of mourning. Freud is not easy here, and Pedder notes the shadows and illuminations along the way. He then takes Klein to task over the terminology and the finer tunings of her theory of infant development, and especially the concept of the depressive position. Apart from debating the veracity of the Kleinian assertion of the sophisticated ego at birth, he asks why the idea of the depressive position, in spite of its centrality in modern psychoanalytic theory, has failed to take root in everyday psychological practice among all professionals. Compared with the idea of "defence mechanisms", for instance, which is accepted in general parlance across a number of schools of practice, Pedder thinks the idea of the depressive position does not easily work because the terms of reference remain problematic. Pedder pins his colours to the mast, and, in Winnicott, he locates a likeminded critic.

The foregoing theory about mourning and the general principles of object loss in Klein none the less form a basis for what is a sort of meta-sociology of depression. Pedder revisits the well-known research of the sociologst George Brown about the experience of depression in women and the key vulnerabilities predisposing women to depression, including the loss of mother before the age of eleven. There is some interesting teasing out of the difference between psychotic and neurotic depression, and the circumstances provoking each. Thereafter, there is a sustained debate about how self-esteem has an impact on depression and mourning. He borrows the term "self-esteem" from Brown and, noting Brown's interest in psychoanalysis, makes a sterling effort to render the idea more psychoanalytically exact. Pedder steps beyond psychodynamic therapy and pin-points how theoretical modifications can inform the practice of guided mourning. To a great extent, the ideas developed here about the treatment of unresolved grief might be of value across a range of denominations, including cognitive–behaviour therapy. There is a sort of theoretical gymnastics as the theories come together, and in the end Pedder moves effortlessly from Bowlby to Liebermann, from Reich to Klein, before rounding off rather enigmatically with quotes from C. S. Lewis and Eugene O'Neill.

CHAPTER THREE

Failure to mourn and melancholia

Background

Psychoanalytic ideas are often criticized as speculative, though it is worth noting that a non-analyst like Sir Aubrey Lewis (1967), in his important historical review of melancholia, wrote of psychoanalytic views, "It is idle to gainsay their importance". This paper reviews ideas about depression and mourning from various quarters, particularly from psychoanalytic writings, then from a sociological perspective, and, finally, from some of the work in behavioural psychotherapy on guided mourning. Among the psychoanalytic views considered here are, first, Freud's classic paper "Mourning and melancholia" (1917b). Klein's concept of the "depressive position" is then reviewed in light of Winnicott's modification and his argument that the term should be re-framed as "the stage of concern". In turning to the work of Brown and Harris (1978a), particular attention is given to their finding that the loss of mother through separation or abandonment before the age of eleven predisposes a woman to neurotic depression, and their more remarkable finding that the loss of mother through death, again before the child is age eleven, predisposes the child to psychotic depression. My central theme, close to Winnicott's, will be that where there has been good-enough mothering in childhood, a good-enough internal object will be established which, though threatened by later loss, will enable healthy mourning to take place and a satisfactory internalization of the lost object over time. When there has been some degree of incomplete secure internal object attainment in childhood, later loss will bring difficulties in mourning, possibly leading to depression. The title of the essay, "Failure to mourn and melancholia", is borrowed both from Freud and an idea in a paper on Eugene O'Neill where an important theme in *The Iceman Cometh* is the "failure to mourn leading to chronic depression" (Hamilton, 1976).

On Freud's "Mourning and melancholia"

Freud (1917b) drew attention to the similarities between mourning and melancholia, that it was, "a profoundly painful dejection, cessation of interest in the outside world, loss of the capacity to love and inhibition of all activity". What, in addition, distinguishes melancholia, he suggested, was a lowering of self-regard "to a degree that finds utterance in self-reproach and self-reviling, and culminates in a delusional expectation of punishment". These internal self-criticisms (sometimes externalized in the form of accusing hallucinatory voices) led Freud on to the idea of the "critical agency", later developed into the concept of the superego. Listening to these self-accusations and self-reproaches in his patient's accounts, it struck Freud that, with little modification, they seemed to be redirected from the lost object. He concluded, "So we find the key to the clinical picture: we perceive that the self-reproaches are reproaches against a loved object which have been shifted away from it on the patient's own ego". Freud argued that there followed an identification of the patient's ego with the lost object, or, as he put it in his well-known aphorism, "the shadow of the object falls upon the ego", leading to both ego and object falling under the harsh judgement of the critical agency.

Apart from self-reproach, another factor which Freud thought distinguished melancholia from mourning was ambivalence. The greater the degree of hate that was mixed with the love felt towards the lost object, the more sadistic would be the internalized self-accusations, nowhere seen more clearly than in the internalization of murderous impulses in suicidal thoughts and behaviour. But are these differences between mourning and melancholia, or between normal and abnormal mourning, as clear-cut as Freud suggested? First, the view that ambivalence is only present in pathological states has been criticized by Bowlby as not in keeping with the evidence. On the contrary, Bowlby (1980) suggested

> that evidence derived from studies of the mourning of ordinary adults does not support that view: ambivalence towards the person lost characterises many cases in which mourning follows a healthy course, although it is admittedly both more intense and more persistent in those that develop pathologically. [p. 29]

Second, the idea that internalization of the ambivalently loved object is the cause of problems in melancholia, as Freud had it, appears to suggest that there is no internalization of the lost object in normal mourning, merely a withdrawal of libido in preparation for it to be reinvested in some new object. We must remember though, that this theory was a child of its time; Freud had just written his major paper "On narcissism" (1914c) and was thinking of these pseudopodal-like movements of libido that could be invested in, or withdrawn from, objects. A theory of internal objects and internal object relations was only just beginning with the idea of the critical agency.

It becomes more clear with the development of the concept of the superego, which is, after all, "built up from the internalised representations and standards of parental figures from infancy onwards" (Brown & Pedder, 1979). By 1923, in *The Ego and the Id*, Freud would no longer have been adhering to this difference between mourning and melancholia, that is to say, that internalization of the lost object only occurs in the latter. By now, he had developed further the concept of the superego and how it evolves from infancy onwards. He writes, "the character of the ego is a precipitate of abandoned object-cathexes" (Freud, 1923b). In other words, Freud suggested that we build up an inner world of objects or images from internal representations of past important relationships. And rather than saying (as in "Mourning and melancholia") that the work of mourning consists of giving up attachments to external objects or of withdrawing libido from them, he develops a description that corresponds much more closely to the idea of internal representation. Anyone who has lost someone of importance to them will be familiar with this. After the initial phases of numbness, protest, and despair, if all goes well, and especially if a relationship with the lost person was enjoyed, then one is left with a good internal object, that is to say, memories and experiences of the lost person which are sustaining. This process of internalization in mourning is not only reflected in phases of childhood development, but also in the satisfactory termination of psychodynamic therapy and psychoanalysis, or any form of education or training.

Klein and the depressive position

In Segal's words (1964) "The depressive position has been defined by Melanie Klein as that phase of development in which the infant recognises a whole object and relates himself to this object" (p. 55). That seems a fairly unexceptional statement, the central idea behind which turns up again and again in different language: that a crucial stage occurs in infant development when people are recognised as separate and whole individuals in their own right. Recognizing mother as a whole person, the source of good and bad experiences, heralds the depressive position and the realization by the infant that his own destructive impulses may harm the object that he loves and totally depends on. The infant is now exposed to new feelings, too; "the mourning and pining for the good object felt as lost and destroyed, and guilt; a characteristic depressive experience which arises from the sense that he has lost the good object through his own destructiveness" (ibid., p. 57).

The concept of the depressive position has been a seminal one in psychoanalytic circles, but it does not seem to have passed into the general body of psychological and psychiatric thinking in quite the same way as, for example, the original psychoanalytic concepts of defence mechanisms which also, more generally speaking, have been absorbed into the language of everyday life. One could think of several possible reasons for the failure of the "depressive position" to become embedded in the general parlance of psychiatry and mental health theory, such as the tendency in Kleinian writings to date phenomena earlier than seems neuro-physiologically plausible, for example, "In Melanie Klein's view, sufficient ego exists at birth to experience anxiety, use defence mechanisms and form primitive object-relations in phantasy and reality" (ibid., p. 11); or the tendency to relate phenomena to the death instinct, for example, "The immature ego of the infant is exposed from birth to the anxiety stirred up by the inborn polarity of instincts—the immediate conflict between the life instinct and the death instinct" (ibid., p. 12); or perhaps people sometimes take exception to the moral or even puritan overdoses in the idea that depression needs to be worked through without recourse to drugs, a necessary dark night of the soul. As Joffe and Sandler (1965) have stated, "We deplore the tendency among some analysts to elevate depression to the status of a virtue without regard to the distinction between the mastery of pain in an adaptive way and the depressive response and melancholia". The very expression "depressive position" appears to refer to a fixed point in time when a variety of highly complicated psychological changes are supposed to take place almost simultaneously, which seem to be an over-simplified condensation of a number of different facets of development which extend over varying lengths of time.

Yet, despite all these criticisms, there is something of importance in the concept that we can see corresponding to similar phenomena that has been otherwise presented in different language. Melanie Klein first developed the concept of the depressive position in her 1934 paper; "A contribution to the psychogenesis of manic depressive states". It was a natural sequel to ideas of both Freud and Abraham. Freud (1917b) was linking the idea of the introjection of the then lost object in melancholia with the concept of regression to an oral phase of libidinal development: "The ego wants to incorporate this object into itself, and, in accordance with the oral or cannibalistic phase of libidinal development in which it is, it wants to do so by devouring it" (p. 249). By the time of Mrs Klein's second major paper in this area, "Mourning and its relation to manic–depressive states" in 1940, her thinking has moved on and less is heard of the concept of oral regression. Now the major developmental shift is seen as before and after the onset of the depressive position, which comes to occupy a central position in her thought.

The satisfactory negotiation of this stage, with the establishment of good internal objects, will determine the future course of mental health and, in particular, the vulnerability to depression in the face of loss later in life. As Klein states, "My contention is that the child goes through states of mind, comparable to the mourning, of the adult, or rather that this early mourning is revisited whenever grief is experienced in later life" (1940, p. 311). Through good early experiences, the infant establishes in its inner world good internal objects or representations of mother and other caring figures. It is interesting to note in passing that Klein emphasized the importance of real external factors here far more than some of her followers appear to have done. On the other hand, Winnicott (1962) has said, in a tone of some exasperation, that though she claimed to have paid full attention to the environmental factor, in his opinion she was "temperamentally incapable" of doing so.

When the actual loss of a loved person occurs in later life, it reactivates the threat of loss of good internal objects. One of the differences, Klein suggested, between the early depressive position and normal mourning is that whereas the baby has his real mother available to help him through the grief he experiences at the loss of breast or bottle,

> with the grown-up person however the grief is brought about by the actual loss of an actual person; yet help comes to him against this overwhelming loss through his having established in his early life his good other inside himself. (Klein, 1940, p. 329]

Anyone familiar with Winnicott's writing will recognize how close this is to his statement that

> the capacity to be alone is based on the experience of being alone in the presence of someone (that is to say, originally mother), and that without a sufficiency of this experience the capacity to be alone cannot develop. [Winnicott, 1958, p. 33]

One might say much the same of the capacity to mourn, that we are not overwhelmed by loss if a good-enough internal object is present.

Loss in later life, then, is a test of the strength of good internal objects, which are threatened each time an actual loss occurs. Klein compares her views with those of Freud and Abraham. At first, as we have seen, Freud had spoken of internalization only in melancholia. Abraham suggested such processes also operate in the work of normal mourning. He concluded that in this work the individual succeeds in establishing the lost loved person in his ego, while the melancholic has failed to do so. Klein goes further:

> My experience leads me to conclude that, while it is true that the characteristic feature of normal mourning is the individual's setting up the lost loved object inside himself, he is not doing so for the first time but, through the work of mourning, is reinstating that object as well as all his loved internal objects which he feels he has lost. He is therefore recovering what he had already attained in childhood. [Klein, 1940, p. 330]

It is the rebuilding of this inner world that characterizes the successful work of mourning. The depressive and the person who fails in the work of mourning have been unable in early childhood to establish their good internal objects and to feel secure in their inner world when threatened with external loss. An inherent implication of Kleinian thinking is that whether or not an individual has traversed the divide between the paranoid–schizoid and the depressive positions determines whether in later life he may become psychotic or neurotic. The fixation point of psychotic illnesses is said to be in the paranoid–schizoid position, whereas "if the depressive position has been reached and at least partially worked through, the difficulties encountered in the later development of the individual are not of a psychotic, but of a neurotic nature" (Segal, 1964, p. 61).

Could this suggested differing predisposition to psychotic or neurotic breakdown help us when we come to consider George Brown's findings of the differing life experiences of women who develop psychotic or neurotic depressive breakdowns? Hard to see how it could, if a very fixed and narrow view is taken of the early dating of the depressive position in the second quarter of the first year of life, as suggested by Klein, which may be one of the reasons already mentioned why the concept may not have become more generally acceptable. But, as Segal says a little further on, "The depressive position is never fully worked through". Or, as Jaques

(1965) says, facing one's own coming death in the mid-life crisis demands a re-working through of the infantile depressive position. The essence of the concept of the depressive position is that it heralds the beginning of processes of internalization of whole internal objects. If one takes the view that this process continues throughout childhood before it is anywhere near completion, then there may be a way of understanding Brown's findings about the effect of loss of mother up to eleven. The Kleinian idea would be that the fixation point of psychotic illness lies in the paranoid–schizoid position before the depressive position is reached, and that when regression takes place in these early stages the individual becomes psychotic. Could it be that in the woman whose mother dies before she is in the depressive position, or internalization of mother is not fully established, depression takes a psychotic form, whereas when the mother is lost through separation, the more protesting form of neurotic depression occurs?

I have made it clear that one ground for objection to the idea of the depressive position might be its very early dating; another would be linking it with the notion of the death instinct. Similar points have been made, among others, by Zetzel and Winnicott. However, as Zetzel (1970) argues, it is possible to accept the fundamental idea of the depressive position without accepting all Melanie Klein's views about a primary death instinct or the very early dating of the Oedipal complex.

As mentioned earlier, another objection to the idea of the depressive position may be to the very name itself, perhaps because it suggests illness rather than health. Winnicott, in writing of similar phenomena, preferred to talk of the capacity for concern in order to emphasize the positive, rather than the negative, side of the same experiences, that is to say, that the infant is beginning to care about and feel responsible for what happens to the object. Winnicott (1962) felt the term "depressive position" to be problematic because it did not emphasize sufficiently the achievement of this stage. He writes, "here being depressed is an achievement, and implies a high degree of personal integration, and an acceptance of responsibility for all the destructiveness that is bound up with living, with the instinctual life, and with anger at frustration" (p. 176).

Winnicott was also critical of the too early dating of the depressive position, giving his view that

> So much of what Klein wrote in the last two decades of her fruitful life may have been spoilt by her tendency to push the age at which mental mechanisms appear further and further back, so that she even found the depressive position in early weeks. [p. 177]

What was essential to Winnicott about the timing of the depressive position, or, as he preferred to call it, the stage of concern, was that it occurred at a phase of two-body relationship before the stage of three person, or Oedipal, relationships. He felt it was "difficult to place the beginnings of the depressive position earlier than 8–9 months, or a year", and elsewhere stated,

> there is no need to be precise about timing, and indeed most of the processes that start up in early infancy are never fully established, and continue to be strengthened by the growth that continues in later childhood, and indeed in adult life, even in old age. [Winnicott, 1963, pp. 73–74]

The emerging consensus from Klein, Winnicott, and others is that towards the end of the first year the infant is aware of mother as a separate being and concerned about the effect of his impulses on her. If "good-enough mothering" is available to help contain the ambivalent feelings of love and hate, then a good-enough internal mother is achieved.

George Brown and the social origins of depression

We turn now to the major sociological study by Brown and Harris (1978a) of depression among women in Camberwell, and consider some of the main findings from their survey of 114 psychiatric patients and two separate random samples totalling 458 women living in the community. They studied the effects of three factors: vulnerability factors, provoking agents, and symptom formation factors. Though there have been criticisms of their studies, in particular, on methodological and statistical grounds (Tennant & Bebbington, 1978), the research stands up to psychoanalytic conceptualization, which Brown and Harris (1978b) frequently quote as a source of their interest. The provoking agents they studied included life events, such as losing a job, and long-term difficulties, such as husband's unemployment. About one half of the depressed women had experienced a recent severe event of aetiological importance and about one-third had a major difficulty of aetiological importance. Loss and disappointment are the central features of such provoking events, which also always imposed a long-term threat. However, "while almost all the women in Camberwell who developed depression in the year of the survey had a severe event or major difficulty, only a fifth of those with such provoking agents broke down" (p. 173). This led to the consideration of vulnerability factors which predispose to depression, of which there were four. First, the lack of a confiding relationship with husband or other; second, the loss of mother before eleven; third, having three or more children under fourteen living at home; and fourth, lack of employment outside the home.

These vulnerability factors contribute to depression only in the presence of a provoking agent. When the latter is present, the rates of depression climb from ten per cent in those with a confiding relationship (whether employed or not) to sixty-three per cent in those with no intimate relationship, with early loss of mother and/or three or more children under fourteen living at home, but still employed; and to 100 per cent in the last group when unemployed outside the home. So far, we have considered provoking agents and vulnerability factors, but not yet symptom formation factors which can influence both the form and severity of depression. With regard to form of depression, Brown and Harris considered the psychotic–neurotic distinction, which they link with the severity of hopelessness. This dimension is similar to the endogenous–reactive distinction, but preferable, since both the terms endogenous and reactive imply a view of the importance of life events, whereas about three-quarters of both psychotic and neurotic groups had provoking agents, that is to say, a severe event or major difficulty.

Past loss of any kind was found to influence the severity of depression, but early loss of mother (before eleven), which had already been shown to act as a vulnerability factor, had a remarkable effect on the form of depression when "past loss by death" was distinguished from "loss by separation". Loss by death predisposed to psychotic depression and loss by separation to neurotic depression. Moreover, these differences were checked on a series of depressed female patients in the Maudsley Hospital and the differentials were substantiated. I have briefly summarized the three-factor causal model of depression put forward by Brown and Harris. Vulnerability factors provide the background predisposition, but only in the presence of provoking agents do they lead to depression, the form of which is influenced by symptom formation factors. This is the causal model, but how do we account for it in theory?

Brown and Harris suggest that these three factors relate in differing ways to a central experience of hopelessness leading to depression. They go on to say,

> Recognition that loss plays an important role in depression has, of course, been widespread. While a good deal of the extensive research literature has dealt with death, Freud made the point in *Mourning & Melancholia* that the object need not necessarily have died but simply have been lost as an object of love. The way in which we have categorized events follows a similar line of thought. Basically we have seen loss events as the deprivation of sources of value or reward. We now go further to suggest that what is important about such loss for the genesis of depression is that it leads to an inability to hold good thoughts about ourselves, our lives, and those close to us. [1978a, p. 233]

The generalization of hopelessness, they believe, forms the central core of depressive disorder. But why do so few people develop such hopelessness in response to life events? This depends on a person's sense of self-esteem and mastery. If both are low before a major loss or disappointment, a woman is less likely to be able to imagine herself emerging. It is this, Brown and Harris believe, that makes sense of the various vulnerability factors in bringing about depression in the presence of severe events and major difficulties. They may seem an odd assortment: loss of mother before eleven, three or more children under fourteen at home, absence of a confiding relation, and lack of employment, but "low self-esteem is the common feature behind all four and it is this that makes sense of them" (*ibid.*, p. 236). Brown and Harris appear to have no difficulty in understanding from their sociological perspective the effect on self-esteem of the three vulnerability factors which all concern the women's present environment, but loss of mother before eleven they find more difficult to explain. However, they do suggest that loss of mother before eleven may have an enduring influence on a woman's sense of self-esteem and mastery.

But what is self-esteem? Does not the very expression of itself acknowledge that it is a two-person relationship; the esteem in which one part of the self is held by another part of the self, or, in other words, an internal object relationship, the sense of esteem or value in which the self is held by internal objects, whether they are called Freud's critical agency, superego, or internal parental imagoes? Little is said by Brown and Harris about these internal aspects of self-esteem, perhaps, as already mentioned, because of their sociological perspective or scientific caution in entering speculative fields. However, the idea of internalization is not far away when they state, in relation to why two of the current vulnerability factors (that is having children at home and no unemployment outside) should lower self-esteem, "The relatively low status attributed to the work of child-care can sometimes be internalized by the women in terms of feelings of low self esteem" (*ibid.*, p. 239).

Brown and Harris liken their notion of a sense of mastery and self-esteem to Bowlby's (1973) concept of self-reliance, which is built up through the security provided by attachment figures, and to Klein's idea of the introjection of a good object, though Bowlby himself also pays rather less attention to the inner world than some other psychoanalytic writers, notably Klein. These four vulnerability factors, then, if present, contribute to the lowering of self-esteem; the reverse also applies: that their absences serve as protective factors to promote self-esteem. Against this background, the state of self-esteem will determine the response to provoking agents such as loss. When self-esteem is high, loss will lead to appropriate grief and resolution; when self-esteem is low, loss leads to failure to work through grief, to hopelessness and depression. Brown and Harris suggest that early loss of mother before eleven, in addition to imparting enduring feelings of low self-esteem, will interfere with the capacity to mourn. There is some evidence that until children are about ten years old they do not readily mourn, although they can be taught how to do so (Furman, 1974). If we hypothesize that the way a person will react to later losses will be influenced by their earlier experiences of loss, it seems plausible that a woman with a loss of mother before eleven will be more likely to fail to work through her later grief. The capacity of children to mourn before ten or eleven remains an open question. Bowlby (1980) suggests it has been underestimated, and that what commonly happens is that children are not given the opportunity of mourning, but are protected by those around in their supposed best interests. I would stress that the internalization of mother is not completed in any early specific period, as Kleinian views of the depressive position might suggest, but goes on throughout childhood, so only after age ten or eleven is there a good enough internal mother to help cope with mourning.

Finally, among Brown and Harris's findings is the question of the effect of type of past loss on the form of depression. All types of past loss affected severity of depression, but loss of mother before eleven by death predisposed to psychotic depression, and loss by separation to neurotic depression. They suggest that loss by death leads to a sense of abandonment and retarded hopelessness, whereas after separation the situation seems less irredeemable, but gives rise to a sense of rejection and protesting despair. This links with Bowlby's (1973) view that a child separated from an attachment figure shows distress in three recognizable phases: protest, despair, and detachment.

Morbid grief and guided mourning

The same phases of protest and despair are also seen later in life in response to bereavement, preceded by another phase of numbness and followed by a final phase of reorganization. The phase of protest, Bowlby has suggested, represents the child's attempts to re-contact his attachment figure. It makes sense that loss of mother before eleven by separation should lead to a cognitive set of protest at being rejected, whereas loss by death leads to a deeper despair of never refinding a good object, either outside or within. The phase of protest and search for the lost object in both infancy and adulthood is accompanied by the subjective state of pining. This experience of pining is emphasized by writers on grief from all sides. Thus, Melanie Klein (1940) wrote of pining for the lost object in the depressive position. Parkes (1972) sees it as the "characteristic feature of the pang of grief". During this phase of pining it is not uncommon for widows, for example, to experience a sense of the presence of the deceased, or even frank hallucination of them, but, as grief work proceeds and the reality of the changes is painfully grasped, a moment comes when the pining gives way to bittersweet nostalgia and recollection of the lost object. The object is now found internally, just when hope is given up of ever meeting again externally. C. S. Lewis (1966) in *A Grief Observed* describes this very well:

> And suddenly at the very moment when, so far, I mourned H. least, I remembered her best. Indeed it was something (almost) better than memory; an instantaneous, unanswerable impression. How easily I might have misjudged another man in the same situation? I might have said, He's got over it. He's forgotten his wife when the truth was he remembers her better because he has partly got over it. [p. 37]

There are several particular clinical situations that must be familiar to many psychotherapists that reflect this protesting state of affairs and make mourning for the lost person very difficult. One is when a parent absents themselves by suicide; another when one marital partner is left unwillingly by the other; or when a therapist abandons a patient without due warning. In all such cases, there is a special problem to internalize any good version of the departing person without considerable defensive distortion.

Recent approaches by behavioural psychotherapists (Lieberman, 1978; Mawson, Marks, Ramm, & Stern, 1981; Ramsay, 1977) to the treatment of morbid grief by guided mourning have provided an interesting bridge between dynamic and behavioural psychotherapy. This approach "likens unresolved grief to other forms of phobic avoidance, which have been treated successfully by exposure to the avoided situation" (Mawson, Marks, Ramm, & Stern, 1981). During treatment patients are "exposed to avoided or painful memories, ideas or situations, both in imagination and in real life, related to loss of the deceased"—such as, for example, the cemetery, or photographs or possessions of the deceased. Such guided mourning "involves an intensive reliving of avoided painful memories and feelings associated with bereavement". All these authors emphasize that painful grief work must be done, likening guided mourning to flooding in the treatment of phobias, but, whereas "systematic desensitization has been shown to be effective with phobics, for grief we have found no gentle equivalent" (Ramsay, 1977).

But what is the essence of this grief work, which, in practical terms, may consist of visits to the cemetery, looking at a photograph of the deceased, or holding a possession of the deceased and then throwing it in the dustbin. The therapeutic technique described sounds very reminiscent of Freud's description of the work of normal mourning in "Mourning and melancholia", when he says "Each single one of the memories and situations of expectancy which demonstrate the libido's attachment to the lost object is met by the verdict of reality that the object no longer exists" (Freud, 1917b, p. 255). It looks almost as if treatment by guided mourning had taken up and developed this statement. However, it must be recalled, as pointed out above, that Freud was writing here of these detachments of libido before the development of his theory of internal objects. It has often happened in the history of psychoanalysis, and psychotherapy derived from it, that a method of therapy emphasizes one aspect, present at some time in the history of psychoanalytic therapy, while neglecting others (see Brown & Pedder, 1979, pp. 166–179). For example, movements such as Reich's bioenergetic therapy can be seen as a development of Freud's first anxiety theory (which he later abandoned); that symptoms are the consequence of dammed-up libido, so that discharge of pent-up feelings and sexual energy was all that was necessary in treatment. This is not only a theoretical extension of Freud's first anxiety theory, but also a therapeutic extension of his early cathartic model of psychotherapy in the *Studies in Hysteria* (Breuer & Freud, 1895d), when Freud used rather surgical metaphors in speaking of the release of strangulated affects. Catharsis certainly plays a part in most types of analytical psychotherapy and it is meant as no criticism of guided mourning to say that it appears to concentrate on release of strangulated affects.

What seems to be left out of the behavioural account, as out of Freud's earlier account of the work of mourning quoted from "Mourning and melancholia", is what is happening in the mourner's inner world. However, the concept of guided mourning does seem to suggest a bridge between dynamic and behavioural psychotherapies and some authors, for example Lieberman (1978), also make use of dynamic concepts. Lieberman (1978) writes that the therapist needs to emphasize his willingness and ability to tolerate without rancour or reproach all the mixed positive and negative feelings the bereaved person has had towards the deceased. This is certainly emphasizes the psychodynamic of therapist's personal contribution to therapy. The patient with morbid grief comes with an incapacity to tolerate ambivalent feelings towards the deceased; the therapist brings his capacity and willingness to do so. Further, I would suggest that the patient suffering from morbid grief does not have good enough internal objects to help him tolerate this ambivalence; the therapist provides him with such a relationship and another chance to internalize and re-establish such an internal object.

Discussion and conclusions

Is it possible to connect up in a single pattern the threads of all the views so far considered? Are they all implied by my early quote from Winnicott (1954) that if the depressive position, or stage of concern, has been satisfactorily negotiated, the reaction to loss is grief, but when it has not, the reaction to loss is depression? The central idea was already present in Abraham (1924): that the predisposition to depression arises in childhood from early disappointments in the child's relationships with its parents. Good enough infant care promotes the establishment of good internal objects and lays the foundations for self-esteem. Disappointment in manageable doses (Jacobson) or gradual disillusionment (Winnicott) "are useful in immunizing the child against the much larger doses of disappointment, anxiety and frustration that he is bound to be exposed to later in life" (Mendelson, 1974). The concept of the depressive position, or stage of concern, is useful if its dating is not rigidly fixed too early. As Dare and Holder (1981) observed, linking it with the development of self-esteem,

> much of what Melanie Klein conceptualized as the "depressive position" and attributed to the child in the second half of the first year is, in our view, more accurately allocated to the second year of life, forming part of the "crisis" of self-esteem at that time. [p. 330]

The importance of self-esteem, we have seen, is central to the theory advanced by Brown and Harris to account for their causal model of depression. The role of self-esteem in protecting against depression is a strong theme running through the writings of ego psychologists (Bibring, 1953). Joffe and Sandler (1965), in particular, see depression as one response to an intolerable state of psychic pain arising when the discrepancy between the actual state of the self and an ideal state of well-being becomes unbearable. When self-esteem is low, this discrepancy between actual and ideal self becomes too unbearably great and a feeling of helplessness and of being unable to restore the wished for state leads to depression. In Brown's words, self-esteem is inadequate for mastery of the disappointment or loss. When loss is further complicated by ambivalence towards the lost object, internal objects are threatened and, if insecurely established in the first place, may be inadequate to meet the threat of further hostile feelings, which have to be denied or disowned. In the presence of an accepting figure, for example, the therapist in guided mourning, there is a new chance to face ambivalent feelings once more and to restore or establish better internal objects. Furthermore, lost objects can only be mourned and satisfactorily internalized when they are accepted as dead. This is Lewis's (1976) point when he observes that mothers of still-born children can only mourn when they have seen the dead baby—when it is "brought back to death". C. S. Lewis found he remembered his wife best as he gave up pining for her. Eugene O'Neill presented his third wife with the manuscript of his autobiographical play, *Long Day's Journey into Night*, on their twelfth anniversary and wrote, "I meant it as a tribute to your love and tenderness which gave me faith in love that enabled me to face my dead at last and write this play" (Hamilton, 1976).

Commentary (GW) on
Chapter Four: Fear of dependence
in therapeutic relationships

In this chapter, Pedder argues the case that all professionals ought to have some theoretical underpinning to the task of understanding patient needs and dependencies. This chapter gives some scope to reflect on the urge in the National Health Service (NHS) to prevent patients from becoming dependent and institutionalized. Pedder's argument is something of a riposte to the dominant opinion during the last decades of the twentieth century, when dependency somehow came to be seen as a bad thing. Especially in psychiatry, care in the community was put into practice with the closure of hospitals and decantation of patients. Part of the rationale for these hospital closures was that mentally ill patients were thought to become unnecessarily institutionalized by the psychiatric system, that somehow the system caused patients to become dependent. Pedder tells us that it is all well and good trying to make patients independent, but what about the process of getting there?

Dr Melanie Bowden, a consultant psychiatrist, notes that there is much in this chapter that has relevance for all mental health workers, as well as psychotherapists and counsellors, and especially including those working in acute psychiatry:

All therapeutic structures can work with and think about healthy dependency or they can defend against it. The chapter is very useful in thinking about dependency and modern psychiatric teams. These teams have the task of containing large amounts of madness and distress. The teams often no longer have the "concrete container" of the institution of the old style mental hospital. They are subject to high degrees of change and challenges to their resources. Within this context certain therapies can come under attack such as long term dynamic therapy. Such therapies can be seen as indulgent and wasteful. Pedder reminds us that long term therapy is important for some patients. It may be helpful to think of dependency/independence as a spectrum rather than an all or nothing; a spectrum along which we progress as we mature, though throughout life we may move forwards and backwards along. Some patients will need to depend before they can move forward and they need sufficient time to move through these stages in therapy. The language and theory of Attachment are useful here in thinking in a non-pejorative way about the patient's attachment experience and how this influences relations with others, including professionals. Some patients will remain at a level of dependence that is disabling, i.e. remain dependent on professionals at least intermittently for social or psychological support and this needs to be acknowledged. If an institution cannot work through its fear of the dependent patient (and its resources being overwhelmed by need) then it may act out against him. This can be expressed through premature discharge or labelling of the patient as "bad" rather than "ill" or "troubled". In psychological therapies this can become the repeated offer of short term therapies. The patient's original trauma is often disturbed or disrupted attachment and when repeated short therapies are offered without thought that the original trauma of repeated short attachment and then abandonment can be reproduced or repeated. The patient is given the double bind message that these short therapies are for his own good and will help. Worse still, he can end up feeling blamed for his inability to respond to the therapy. Repeating bad attachment experiences through "help" in this way, often compounds the problem causing a vicious cycle for the patient where he is forced to cling to the structure which gives him this confusing message. The patient may unconsciously use increasingly dysfunctional behaviour such as self harm or escalating symptomotology to get more "help". [personal communication]

Pedder's argument is that dependency is necessarily phasic, and, unless it is carefully worked through, the patient will be unable to overcome his dependency needs. He offers us a clear solution to the management of very needy patients: he tells us to embrace their dependency, work with it and work through it, and the rewards will come. In the end, he asks, what's wrong with dependency anyway? It is not quite a political counterpoise to the attack on the so-called "nanny-state" by those on the right, who have claimed that the welfare state is too soft, but Pedder notably refers us to the cultural climate in the UK, where the idea of independence has been over-esteemed. Pedder points out that the idea of dependency is viewed very differently elsewhere in the world and that we might do well to embrace a broader conception of it. He notes, in particular, the Japanese concept of "amaeru", which means "to depend or presume upon another's love". Pedder observes how this notion is resonant with Balint's idea of "primary love" and that if therapy begins with this presumed, the acceptance of dependency has an entirely different quality. The chapter unfolds a dense theoretical exposition of the idea of dependency that runs through the work of Balint, Fairbairn, Guntrip, and Anna Freud, among others. Fairbairn's indispensable idea of the shift from infantile to mature dependency is situated herein. Fairbairn posits that independence is really a myth; we grow towards a state of an acceptance of our dependency on others, rather than becoming independent. For Fairbairn, dependency is not a state to be avoided; rather, it is one of realizing our reliance on others, that we are best realizing how we continue to rely on others even throughout our adult life. As Melanie Bowden points out, some modern NHS psychiatric services, like those that have developed a recovery approach (Repper & Perkins, 2003) begin with an acceptance of the role of managing dependencies:

> In understanding how to work with dependency in chronic illness and mental distress, ideas coalescing around the recovery model, and its emphasis on shared responsibility, can be helpful. Arguably dependency frameworks are accepted in some modern health care approaches, for instance in therapeutic community settings and increasingly in complex need services. This is a very positive step. Here dependency is acknowledged and worked with not as a pure

problem, weakness or stigma but as one part of the human firmament. Such cultures might emphasise mutual learning and a belief in shared experience. Pedder's chapter reminds us of the importance of understanding these issues and brings them into sharper distinction in the work we do. [personal communication]

Reference

Repper, J., & Perkins, R. (2003). *Social Inclusion & Recovery*. London. Balliere & Tindall.

Fear of dependence in therapeutic relationships

Introduction

I n this paper, I consider the fear of dependence, as it is experienced by therapists and patients in therapeutic relationships. The concept of dependence is briefly reviewed in both Eastern and Western psychoanalytic literature. A clinical illustration is given of the fear of dependence in a male patient. It is suggested that the Western ideal of independence is a myth which especially ignores the reliance on internal others. Although this chapter is mainly about the fear of dependence experienced by patients, the ideas I want to explore first came from thinking about the fears experienced by clinicians in relation to patients becoming dependent on them, or on the institutions in which they work.

Twice during my career, I have worked in newly opened psychiatric units in district general hospitals and have noticed how frustrated, irritated, and resentful some staff can become when patients do not improve as had been hoped and expected over several months. The opening of new units in the UK in the latter part of the twentieth century to replace older mental hospitals was heralded with a great new mood of hope and optimism: we were going to get away from the old custodial methods of mental hospitals; patients were going to be made better, quickly; they were going to go home, out into the community; and all would be different. These units attracted psychiatric staff with a great deal of therapeutic enthusiasm and they attracted younger people who wished to see a change from the old custodial methods. We have seen similar movements in other countries; the Italian experience, for instance, where old ideas were overhauled in a long-overdue system change away from former methods.

However, in these units there were still some patients who failed to improve, and, at times, some staff seemed to resent this. There are no doubt many factors that might account for that resentment— there may be a failure of therapeutic ideals, optimism, and hope, and this threatens the sense of therapeutic potency in all of us. But another factor is considered here, which is the threat experienced by the staff of dependence of patients on them. Martindale (1989) describes this problem in relation to providing physical and mental care for elderly patients. Based on his experience of a multi-disciplinary seminar group for mental health professionals, Martindale emphasizes the fears of both the elderly persons and their younger therapists, particularly when the elderly patients are near to the age of the therapist's own elderly relatives. In many areas of medicine—especially in acute medicine and surgery—it is, of course, normal for patients to become temporarily dependent on the hospital and the staff looking after them. They regress to a more childlike state, becoming dependent upon the doctors and nurses, evoking a familiar transference where professionals are experienced in light of parental roles, as if being looked after by "fathers and mothers". This transference is normally reversible and creates no difficulties. It was Tom Main (previously director of the Cassel therapeutic community in Richmond) who said that you knew when men in a surgical ward were beginning to get better, because they started to flirt with the nurses, that is, when they were acutely ill and unwell they were very happy to be looked after by the angel–nurse— desexualized mother, but as soon as they began to get better, that state was reversed: they resumed their adult ways of behaviour, including flirting with the nurses.

That kind of regression in the transference, and subsequent return to the adult state, is normal in much of acute medicine and surgery, but the situation becomes very different in chronic care of any kind, and particularly in chronic psychiatric care. In new psychiatric units, the idea that patients should get better seemed to be grounded in a wish that chronic dependency could be avoided. There are various ways in which institutions have tried to avoid dependent patients. One common method in psychiatry, in the UK and elsewhere, is by the rotation of staff, for example, the rotation of junior doctors every six months. There are many rationalizations for that. We say it is necessary for the training of the doctors to have a range of experiences; but I think there are other factors involved, such as the avoidance of fostering dependent relationships. The same may be said of rotational nursing systems; there are possibly good educational, practical, and political reasons why we rotate staff, but one of the things it attempts to avoid is patients becoming too dependent. Psychiatric treatment might be said to be set up in a way that the patient's need for dependency is never actually confronted or resolved and is, instead, inadvertently perpetuated by the system.

Sometimes, by contrast, we recognize and accept the necessity for dependence, and because we know it is too great for any individual to bear, we allow it to develop in relation to the institution itself or what it represents. If individuals, especially newcomers to psychiatry, are to feel comfortable with the dependent needs of patients, they need the help of someone to turn to themselves for regularly available support and supervision, rather as mothers of first-born infants need the support of their own mother, partner, or health visitor. It is from this perspective that we might begin to think about professionals' fears of dependence. We may, hereupon, review the concept of dependence, which, in our literature, is more concerned with fears of dependence as experienced by patients.

Western and Eastern assumptions of dependency

In general, the idea of dependence is looked on with disfavour in the West, at any rate in recent centuries, as contrary to the Protestant work ethic. On the other hand, independence is valued throughout the West. In the USA, we have the Declaration of Independence, the War of Independence, Independence Day. In the UK, a new newspaper was started called the *Independent*. Within the British Psychoanalytical Society, we have the Independent group, where we like to think we are independent of the dogma of either Freud or Klein. Bion's (1961) concept of "basic assumption" groups comes to mind here. The work of any group may be interfered with by three basic assumptions: dependency, fight/flight, and pairing. He compared these with three institutions, respectively, the Church, the Army, and the aristocracy. In the dependent assumption group, as illustrated by the Church, there is a reliance on the omnipotent figure of God: although, as Bion points out, there is always a paradox in that although one is supposed to depend on God's help it must never be acted on—you still have to provide for yourself.

So, in the West, there seems to be an idea that independence is good and dependence is bad. Bowlby (1969) especially has commented on the concept of dependence and compared it with his preferred concept of attachment. As he points out, there is a paradox that dependence and attachment mean roughly similar things, and independence and detachment mean roughly similar things, yet they have very different connotations. We think attachment in relationships is good, though dependence is rather bad; we think independence good and detachment rather bad. He writes, in the first volume of *Attachment and Loss*,

> It will be noticed that in this account the terms "dependence" and "dependency" are avoided, although they have for long been in common use by psychoanalysts and also by psychologists who favour a theory of secondary drive. The terms derive from the idea that a child becomes linked to his mother because he is dependent on her as the source of physiological gratification . . . The fact is that to be dependent on a mother-figure and to be attached to her are very different things. Thus, in the early weeks of life an infant is undoubtedly dependent on his mother's ministrations, but he is not yet attached to her. [1958, p. 278]

And, further on, he says,

> As a consequence of these different meanings, we find that, whereas dependence is maximum at birth and diminishes more or less steadily until maturity is reached, attachment is altogether absent at birth and is not strongly in evidence until after an infant

is past six months. The words are far from synonymous. . . . A common judgement is that for a person to be dependent is less good than for him to be independent: in fact, to call someone dependent in his personal relations is usually rather disparaging. But to call someone attached is far from disparaging. On the contrary, for members of a family to be attached to one another is regarded by many as admirable. Conversely, for a person to be detached in his personal relations is commonly regarded as less than admirable. [*ibid.*, p. 279]

So, Bowlby seems keen to displace the concept of dependence by that of attachment, even though, as he points out, they really relate to different phases and are not exactly complementary. Perhaps he is also following the Western tradition of considering dependence bad and independence good. Birtchnell (1984, 1988) has commented on this discrepancy in Bowlby when reviewing his work and that of others. Birtchnell (1984) distinguishes three major components of dependence: affectional, ontological, and deferential, the first of which corresponds to Bowlby's concept of anxious attachment. He considers the contribution of dependence to proneness to depression and the important intervening link of self-esteem. This parallels the emphasis on self-esteem in vulnerability to depression in the work of George Brown (Brown & Harris, 1978). As noted before (Pedder, 1985), the concept of self-esteem itself implies an internal object relationship—the esteem in which one part of the self is held by another. Birtchnell, too, suggests that anxiously attached or affectionally dependent patients lack an adequately internalized loving parent, which diminishes what Winnicott (1958) called their capacity to be alone (see Conclusion, below).

Neki (1976), from India, in an interesting article concerning "dependence in social and therapeutic relationships", reviewed the cultural relativism of the concept of dependence. He described two distinct developmental patterns: the West fostering independence and, by contrast, India allowing dependence and valuing dependability. He points out that, in general terms, the Western tradition is a more urban one while the Indian one is more rural (though that must be changing):

In contradistinction to independence as the developmental goal in Western societies, Indian society seems to posit dependability as the developmental goal . . . For Western children, even the period of biologically necessitated dependence also is made as brief as possible—so that they may be able to enjoy their independence for as long a period as they can. As children grow up, they quickly become independent of parents. They have their separate bed-rooms, separate social groups and separate activities . . . In fact, the Indian culture tends to foster dependence right from birth. The infant stays and sleeps in the same bed as the mother—in close physical contact with her almost all the time. Mothering is indul-gent, uninterrupted and prolonged. There is no hurry to wean chil-dren off the breast. [*ibid.*, p. 5]

Moving still further East in considering the cultural relativism of how dependence is valued, Doi (1973) has written from Japan of the concept of "amaeru", which he describes as an intransitive verb meaning "to depend or presume upon another's love"; this may describe the relationship between a mother and her child, and also one that is socially sanctioned between two adults. Balint (1965) commented that European languages seem to have no words to express what he was trying to get at in his concept of primary object love:

In one respect, however, all European languages are the same— again as far as I know them. They are all so poor that they cannot distinguish between the two kinds of object-love, active and passive. [*ibid.*, p. 56]

And he later drew attention (Balint, 1968) to Doi's work:

Before going further, I wish to refer here to some clinical and linguistic observations of Doi (1962). According to him, there exists in Japanese a very simple, everyday word, amaeru, an intransitive verb, denoting "to wish or to expect to be loved" in the sense of primary love. "Amae" is the noun derived from it, while the adjec-tive "amai" means "sweet". These words are so common that indeed the Japanese find it hard to believe that there is no word for amaeru in the European languages. [*ibid.*, p. 69]

More recently, Doi (1989) said that he had stumbled on the concept of amae in treating Japanese patients psychoanalytically, being struck by the fact that their relationship to the therapist is tinged with the same emotional tone which pervades all interpersonal relationships in Japan, the quality that can best be described by the Japanese word amae. This word, he says,

> . . . primarily describes the behaviour and its accompanying affect of a child seeking his mother or any caring person; but it may refer to the similar situations that occur between adults. Amae in its most primitive form is equal to the concept of primary love defined by Michael Balint. It also can be related to the concept of attachment elaborated by John Bowlby. [*ibid.*, p. 353]

Among Western psychoanalytic authors, Fairbairn and Guntrip have given prominence to the idea of conflict over dependence as the root cause of psychological disturbance. It is worth looking briefly at the history of changing views in the psychoanalytic literature about what is the core conflict in neurosis and other psychological disturbance. Freud first focused on conflicts over sexuality, and he evolved the idea of the Oedipus complex as central in all neurosis. But it is a common popular misrepresentation of Freud to assume that he attributed all problems to sex, and, thereby, to dismiss psychoanalysis as culture-bound to bourgeois Vienna of the 1880s and not of general relevance. Indeed, as we know, Freud found that many of his female hysterical patients were suffering from sexual conflicts, but it is instructive to note his actual words in "The neuro-psychoses of defence" (Freud, 1894a):

> In all the cases I have analysed it was the subject's sexual life that had given rise to distressing affect . . . Theoretically, it is not impossible that this affect should sometimes arise in other fields; I can only report that so far I have not come across any other origin. [*ibid.*, p. 52]

Since then, of course, we have indeed come to recognize the immense importance of conflict "in other fields", for example, over-aggressive feelings, which may be turned against the self (in depression and suicidal attempts) or converted into psychosomatic symptoms. I have commented before (Pedder, 1987) on the puzzle about how late Freud came to accept the importance of aggression, which he himself, later in life, said surprised him.

So we have, in historical sequence, an emphasis on conflicts over sexuality, followed by conflicts over aggression, and then, by

Fairbairn, Guntrip, and others, conflicts over dependence. Historical developments in psychoanalytic theory have, therefore, inversely reflected successive stages of development (in classical theory, oral, anal, and Oedipal). Guntrip (1961) suggested that Fairbairn had arrived at one general and fundamental conclusion: that the root cause of all personality disturbance is the unconscious persistence within the adult personality of too strong an element of infantile dependence:

> There is nothing that grown-ups feel to be so humiliating as the "accusation" of childishness (and psychoanalytic interpretations are usually at first felt to be accusations). Adults fear the child in themselves and everything that keeps him alive inside, as a danger to the maintenance of their adult social and vocational roles, and as likely to expose them to unwelcome criticism or even scorn from those who are secretly as afraid as themselves. They deny the existence of the child in the unconscious . . . We are on solid ground in saying that what makes neurosis possible to begin with is the prolonged biological dependence of the human offspring on the parents. [*ibid.*, p. 381]

This prolonged biological dependence of the child on parents has been commented on many times. Anna Freud (1980), in particular, writes of her own father's work:

> Infantile dependency as an agent in character formation . . . is a familiar concept in Freud's writings, where it is dealt with as a "biological fact" and held responsible for almost all the personality gains of the developing human being . . . The long period of the human child's dependency is held responsible by him also for such vital matters as the capacity to form object relationships in general, and the Oedipus complex in particular; the cultural struggle against aggression and the need for religion; in short, for the individual's humanization, socialization, and his ethical and moral needs. [*ibid.*, pp. 43–44]

She gives a whole list of footnotes of where this appears in Freud's writings, from which I give just one example ". . . the biological facts that the young of the human race pass through a long period of dependence and are slow in reaching maturity" (Freud, 1919g, p. 261).

Guntrip (1961) reminds us that Ferenczi was one of the first to recognize, among analysts, the importance of the primary mother–child relationship. Ferenczi, in Budapest, was Melanie Klein's first analyst, before she went to Abraham in Berlin, so that there was a line of succession in emphasizing the importance of the mother, from Ferenczi to Melanie Klein. Guntrip (1961) writes that Freud's theory and practice was notoriously paternalistic; Ferenczi's maternalistic. Ferenczi's concept of "primary object love" prepared the way for the later work of Melanie Klein, Fairbairn, Balint, Winnicott, and all others who today recognize that object relations start at the beginning in the infant's need for the mother.

Balint (1965) believed that the aim of analysis cannot be achieved unless the patient is able to revert to a stage of primary passive love in the transference, which he described as "the new beginning". The recognition that object relations begin with the mother–infant relationship was also the rationale of Ferenczi's mothering technique in analysis (which worried Freud) and of Winnicott's stress on therapeutic regression. Guntrip (1961) discusses the characteristics of pathological dependence in the following terms:

> The extent to which infantile dependent characteristics are allowed to manifest themselves on the level of consciousness and behaviour varies greatly . . . When analysis has the chance to go deep enough it is truly astonishing how powerful and frightening to the patient is the degree of primitive infantile rage, unsatisfied need and intense fear-ridden dependent longing that is revealed. [*ibid.*, p. 390]

As Guntrip says, the work of Winnicott provides an outstanding example of courageous grappling with the implications for analysis of the position that the roots of personality disturbance are to be found in the earliest mother–infant relationship. Winnicott's work as a paediatrician and psychoanalyst enabled him to trace the origins of mental disturbance back to the very beginnings of life in the mother–infant relationship. He held that

> classic psychoanalysis is the correct method for dealing with psycho-neurosis as a problem of the Oedipal situation. By contrast, he speaks of "Management" as the appropriate method for

dealing with regressed and psychotic patients whose problems are on the pre-Oedipal level where good mothering is the supreme desideratum ... The position that seems to be emerging is that at all stages psychotherapy has to be an appropriate mixture of mothering (management) and analysis (giving insight). [Guntrip, 1961, p. 413]

I would rather see it as providing a mixture of female and male, feminine and masculine elements; certainly the analytic psychotherapist has to combine both male and female elements in him- or herself. I had the fortunate experience of working, some years ago, as co-therapist in a psychotherapy group with Joffe, a few years before his death. He combined warm friendly humanity with shrewd analytic insights—a subtle blend of feminine and masculine traits.

Fairbairn (1952) wrote of a two-stage developmental sequence in the maturation of dependence: from infantile dependence ripening into mature dependence. Winnicott (1963) later introduced a three-stage classification of dependence, revising the delineation of dependence and independence by thinking separately of "absolute dependence, relative dependence; and towards independence" (*ibid.*, p. 84). Neki (1976), considering an Indian cultural perspective, contrasted the approach of different groups of psychotherapists towards dependence. He described a first group of Western psychotherapists who would consider dependence a nuisance, rather like the staff I mentioned in my introduction, who felt threatened by dependence. If a patient enters into a more malignant regressed state, such psychotherapists assume that there was a mistaken assessment or diagnosis in the first place: the patient should not be there. Then Neki contrasts

... [a] second group we have already identified—the one that considers dependence as the basic pathology of all psychiatric disorders. In their view the treatment approach necessary is to help the patient go into full clinical regression (Winnicott, 1975); to get behind the infantile dependence (Fairbairn, 1952); and let the patient start from a new beginning (Balint, 1965); to provide him with a model of good object relations (Guntrip, 1961); and, if necessary, gratify the patient's dependent needs by the "mothering technique" (Ferenczi, 1952). [Neki, 1976, p. 18]

Khan (1972c) wrote of his own struggles with this problem and how he attempted to facilitate and meet regression without fostering what Balint (1968) called "malignant regression". I would like to draw attention to the evocative title of Khan's article, "Dread of surrender to resourceless dependence in the analytic situation", which aptly underlines many points. Bollas (1987) has written about the "ordinary regression to dependence", which may be fostered by the analyst's receptivity or arrested by the analyst's interpretations.

The reader may be wondering about the relevance of the above. I think this applies on several levels; in relation to patients' demands; in relation to our need for support and supervision; and in relation to our own therapy and development as therapists. First, in relation to our practice with patients, some brief focal forms of therapy can be effective in helping patients work through dependency issues; however, other patients will need longer periods of therapy that will allow for dependence to emerge and be worked through. Pacing the management of dependency needs in therapy can be very difficult when the parameters of therapy are influenced by training programmes, insurance schemes, or other pressures, such as resource constraints, which allow for only brief periods of treatment. Second, I think it is relevant in relation both to supervision of formal psychotherapy and to staff support in dealing with demanding, dependent patients as described by Martindale (1989). We all, at times, both as trainees and later on, need to ask for help with patients, and to acknowledge our need for somebody else's help. I think this is more difficult as we become more senior, although many analysts and therapists do continue supervision or belong to various kinds of peer groups which offer mutual supervision. Third, it is very relevant for us as therapists in relation to our own therapy or analysis, and whether we pursue that either as an inherent part of training or later when in difficulty. We have to acknowledge our need for somebody else's help, and remember that Freud (1937c), in "Analysis terminable and interminable", proposed that all analysts need re-analysis every five years.

Case history: the myth of independence

I want to describe briefly the treatment of a patient from the helping professions where issues of dependency were extant. Initially, he denied any personal need for psychotherapy, saying he was only pursuing it for professional reasons. He had spent twenty years in a military career; then, in his forties, he had moved on to work in the helping professions. It was as if the Army had earlier catered for the more "macho" masculine side of his personality, but there was another, more feminine, side, that had been unused and frustrated in the services. During his military career he had been an expert in survival techniques: lecturing and running courses on how to survive in solo situations: at the North Pole; in the jungle; or wherever else this might be appropriate. He had been born abroad, in the "evening shadows" of the British Empire. He had a brother, two years younger, whom he had always had to look after. They had been sent away to boarding school. He described it in this way: once a year they went on an extraordinarily long train journey, and they did not come home for nine months. He went to that school from the age of six to fifteen. On the train journey there and back, and at school, he had to look after and defend this younger brother.

At first, in the transference, I was the younger brother who needed looking after and protecting. He found it immensely difficult to trust anyone, including me, for any kind of help or support. He was very reluctant to use the couch; it would have meant to him being a helpless patient, and that meant weakness. He had come to learn about himself, but only for professional reasons. He could not consider coming more than once a week to begin with, and then twice a week after nine months, because of his fear of regression, helplessness, and weakness, particularly if he used the couch: younger people might need it, but not he. Sometimes, I felt sessions were more like supervision than psychotherapy, as if he had come to discuss his patient self, but at arm's length. It reminded me of Winnicott's (1965) statement:

> It is as if a nurse brings a child, and at first the analyst discusses the child's problem, and the child is not directly contacted. Analysis does not start until the nurse has left the child with the analyst, and the child has become able to remain alone with the analyst and has started to play. [p. 151]

So, with this patient, there was a continual problem of resistance to analysis, of fear of weakness, helplessness, and a denial of any dependency needs. His resistance to psychotherapy and the idea of using the couch increased particularly on three separate occasions. The first was during the Falklands crisis, when many of his friends and former military comrades were fighting there. The male part of him identified intensely with them and he thought that would be "very wet" and weak, while his friends were fighting for their lives in the South Atlantic, for him to lie on the couch. After eighteen months, he was able to use the couch regularly and acknowledge his need to get behind these "macho" defences. But, at times, he still thought it was better to die than to be helpless; this was one of the things he used to advise people about on survival courses. There was a tremendous "dread of surrender", particularly to me on the couch, with all its homosexual overtones. There was a second period of retreat from the couch, when his son—then in his late teens—went to the country of his father's birth to retrace his father's childhood. The patient felt he had to be parent to his son in that moment, and could not be more of a child–patient with me. The third episode of retreat was when his own mother became ill and died. He could not possibly be a patient while she needed looking after. It was all right for his younger brother to mourn and miss her, but not for him. Towards the end of psychotherapy, he cut down the frequency of his sessions to once a week again, and it became at times much more like supervision, as at the start, rather than therapy for himself as a patient.

Conclusion

It is a myth of independence that it is actually possible to be wholly independent. Most of us are continually dependent on others in the outside world; even if living alone we rely on the postman, milkman, radio, etc. (apart from a few very bizarre recluses, like survivors of wars in remote places). Indeed, I would argue that even the most independent seeming people are continually dependent on internal others. Mature independence involves this, and echoes Winnicott's (1958) view that "the capacity to be alone is based on the experience of being alone in the presence of someone, [i.e., originally Mother] and that without a sufficiency of this experience the capacity to be alone cannot develop" (*ibid.*, p. 33).

As discussed earlier, if we do not have secure internal objects on whom we can depend, we are more likely to need external others to maintain self-esteem, and we may become depressed when they are not available (Birtchnell, 1984; Pedder, 1985). The problems surrounding fear of dependence are relevant both for our patients and for ourselves as patients or therapists, and as supervisors or supervisees.

Commentary (GW) on Chapter Five: Termination reconsidered

When it comes to the challenge of ending in therapeutic encounters, Pedder has some suggestions as to how the rather bleak notion of "termination" might be reconsidered. Pedder does not actually call Freud to account for the origination of the idea of termination; rather, he questions the way in which it was popularized by followers (see, for example, Bridger, 1950; Klein, 1950). Pedder reviews Freud's original idea of "Die Endliche und die Unendliche Analyse" and argues that it has been prone to problematic translations into the English language. He points out that a translator's choice of the word "termination" might arouse negative connotations, with overtones of "terminal cancer" or "termination of pregnancy". The idea of termination, he argues, does not do justice to the fact that psychoanalytic therapy is concerned with the internalization of healthier ways of being, and that the process of ending becomes a new beginning where the therapy is internalized and therefore ongoing. While not denying the importance of working through phases of disappointment and arriving at a point of a realistic sense of loss, Pedder challenges the psychoanalytic image, perpetuated by patients and practitioners alike, of endings as a foreboding event.

Pedder offers a thorough overview of a range of theories about when is a good time end in therapy. Indeed, the review in this chapter is probably one of the best accounts of finishing in therapy that we have to date. He, radically and disarmingly, it might be said, challenges the orthodox conventions of psychoanalytic practice. First, he recommends the flexibility of a *crescendo–diminuendo* approach to frequency of sessions, against the grain of many of his colleagues. And second, in suggesting that colleagues adopt the term "graduation" in cases where therapy arrives at an agreeable end point negotiated between therapist and patient, Pedder argues that "termination" should be reserved for a forced or premature ending in therapy. The idea of graduation re-casts the more sombre idea of ending or closure, suggesting an altogether more uplifting finality.

It is not entirely certain that Pedder's term "graduation" captures the usually melancholic unforgettableness of ending in psychoanalytic therapy, but it does take us in a different direction. He does not go into the detail of the criteria for therapeutic discharge beyond the notion of symptom diminution, mitigation or elimination of presenting problems, such as thoughts of suicide, but the extant idea is that there is some evidence that clinical improvements will be sustained beyond therapy where the patient has demonstrated sufficient capacity for "enjoyment and efficiency", often translated as a capacity for love and work, as Freud puts it (1917b). In the classical Freudian sense, therapeutic results are considered in terms of the functioning of the ego, that is to say, the ego does not have to expend so much energy in repression and is strengthened for bearing reality. The energy of the id becomes more mobile, the superego more tolerant, and the ego freer of anxiety. Pedder is drawn to Ferenczi's (1927) intuitive idea that the end of therapy is probably due when the therapist feels that the patient has become "unruffled" and able to "free associate easily".

Crucially for Klein (1950), treatment is deemed as completed only when both the positive and negative transference have been worked through. Klein argued that termination of therapy should be given several months' notice in order that the patient has time to undergo the process of mourning. While Klein grants that good progress can be made in a positive transference, fundamentally, she asserts, it is only half the job, and that it is the negative transference where the therapeutic gains are truly made. This emphasis on the working through of the negative transference with Klein, and this is a point that Pedder touches on, does not mean that the therapist has to force the agenda by "being the bad object" (being overly critical for the sake of it, for instance), rather that the therapist is simply available enough for the reception of the patient's projected negative feelings. It is this withholding that is often a character trait of Kleinians, where authority transference is kindled in the place of otherwise socially contrived responses. For example, ordinary greeting (a smile or the shake of the hand) is replaced by a quietened repose. This poise may be perceived as hostile or rejecting, and becomes the root of the patient's disaffection that unfolds the patient's negativity that signals a path to the patient's internal world. Most developmental transitions take place in an uneasy climate. The first steps of the toddling infant are prospecting, but invariably are followed by a fall; the first time the stabilizers are removed, the bike will topple. When an adolescent or young adult leaves home they are ready to leave home, but never completely equipped for what departure entails.

Pedder recommends that, ideally, notice of the end of therapy might follow the rule of thumb that notice should be the square root of the length of treatment (we can call this Pedder's Rule); for example, if you see a patient for nine months, then three months notice is due, if you a client for thirty-six months, then notice should be six months, and so forth. And it is disappointment, rather than hostility, that is the focus of what Pedder sees as the working-through task to the end. Of course, no therapy is ever complete, and endings are always different. At their worst endings should never be a shock because breaks throughout therapy can be dry runs for the final parting, as Bridger (1950) pointed out. At best, therapeutic closure might toll to the tune of "parting as such sweet sorrow", as Pedder is finally moved to show us.

References

Bridger, H. (1950). Criteria for the termination of analysis. *International Journal of Psycho-Analysis*, 31: 202–203.

Ferenczi, S. (1927). The problem of the termination of the analysis. In: *Final Contributions*. London: Hogarth.

Freud, S. (1917b). Mourning and melancholia. *S.E., 14*: 243–258.
Klein, M. (1950). Termination of analysis. In: *Envy & Gratitude* (pp. 43–50). London: Virago.

Termination reconsidered

"The mere termination of breastfeeding is not a weaning"

(Winnicott, 1953)

Introduction

In this paper I want to reconsider the expression "termination". It is suggested that the expression itself is a curiously inappropriate term, with its negative and finite connotations which fail to convey the positive hopes for a new beginning that normally surround the end of a satisfactory analysis. The single word termination does not distinguish the external reality of interruption of visits to the analyst from the internal continuation of the analytic process. Moreover, it ignores the awkward circumstance that analysts, on qualification, often continue to meet their own analyst. The word termination has become so much part of the jargon of psychoanalysis and psychotherapy, but for a long time I have felt it is a rather odd, unsatisfactory, and inappropriate term for what should be a healthy developmental process. It would be naïve of me to imagine that I could abolish it from the literature, because it is so much a received concept now, and I would not even be sure what to replace it with. A number of words suggest themselves, most of which imply something to do with developmental stages: "gradua-tion", "rebirth", "new beginning", "separation–individuation", "renunciation"—and no doubt many others suggest themselves which all have various different resonances. So, why do I think the word is unsatisfactory or wrong? Termination usually refers to something final and irrevocable. We speak of the termination of pregnancy, or of a contract, or of employment. We speak of pests being exterminated, of terminal illness, of railway termini, where there is nothing beyond—a final stop. The fact that we speak of termination of pregnancy underlines what I consider is wrong about the expression, because termination of pregnancy, on the whole, is a fairly negative experience—often it involves a tragedy, or a disaster, either at the time or later in life. There is no new life beyond termination of pregnancy.

Premature termination

Perhaps we can speak of analysis or psychotherapy being termi-nated when it is, as in pregnancy, similarly brought to an end prematurely, for example, if the analyst moves, or dies. Often we do talk about a case being terminated when the therapist has to move to another job. The effect of the analyst's geographical moves has been particularly reviewed by Dewald (1966). Limentani (1982), in a paper on the "unexpected termination of psychoanalytic ther-apy", wrote about six cases from his own practice that had had to be terminated unexpectedly. In a discussion of that paper, compar-isons were made with termination in brief focal psychotherapy (Malan, 1963). It was commented that termination in brief psycho-therapy is very different from what Limentani was talking about, because it should never be unexpected: it should be planned right from the beginning, and so never premature. However, perhaps we could use the word "termination" in either psychotherapy or in pregnancy when the ending is premature and unexpected.

Indeed, what Limentani writes in questioning Dewald's opti-mism about the effect of forced termination in his cases might equally have been written about termination of pregnancy: "I am nevertheless concerned with the inevitable scarring left by the attack on the setting and the very essence of the analytic process caused by the broken trust and promise" (p. 420). Pregnancy normally ends in birth, a new beginning, an externalization of the foetus into the outer world. Analysis, like pregnancy, may be prematurely terminated, but normally ends with an internalization of the analyst into the patient's inner world.

A patient in analysis who was uncertain about whether or not she might have to finish analysis for external reasons, expressed this very well. She said one day that she felt she knew what it must be like to be an embryo, and not know whether or not you are going to be terminated. That also reminded me of the point that Lewis (1976) makes about the problem for a mother of mourning a stillbirth—that the mothers of stillborn babies can mourn only when they have seen the dead baby, when it is, in his phrase, "brought back to death". In the unexpected termination of pregnancy, or of analysis, there is an interference with that normal mourning process.

Background

Although the word "termination" is part of the jargon of analysis or psychotherapy, I was surprised that it does not appear in dictionaries of psychoanalysis such as Laplanche and Pontalis (1973); or in Rycroft (1968); or in the index to standard textbooks like that of Fenichel. In the final, index, volume of the *Standard Edition*, it does not appear in its own right; it only appears under "psychoanalytic treatment, termination of". Almost all the references here are to the Dora case (Freud, 1905e), where analysis was prematurely broken off after three months. Freud writes that "the transference took me unaware", suggesting to him that Dora had broken off treatment at the time of experiencing erotic wishes towards himself because he had failed to point out, in time, the connexion between himself, Herr K, and Dora's father. When erotic feelings for Freud came too near the surface, she broke off analysis and fled from Freud, that is to say, she acted out rather than remembered her wish for revenge on Herr K. And this was one of the experiences that helped Freud to see that transference, far from being an obstacle to treatment, could be an invaluable tool and ally if it was detected and revealed to the patient in time.

In thinking of the whole concept of termination, we naturally think of Freud's (1937c) classic paper, "Analysis terminable and interminable". Here, the German is actually "Die Endliche und die Unendliche Analyse". My German dictionary, under "endliche", gives "final, finite, ultimate". Certainly, they imply something like "terminable", but it might have been translated into English as "Analysis finite and infinite", or "Analysis ending and unending". And Freud is asking the question, after all: "Can analysis end? Is there an end to it?" As we shall see later, he felt perhaps there could only be a true ending in traumatic cases, and also he advised reanalysis every five years—at least for analysts and therapists.

Some of the alternative words I have already suggested imply various developmental stages. In thinking of the end of analysis or psychotherapy, it is natural to compare it with various developmental stages: birth, weaning, separation–individuation, adolescence, leaving home. All these are naturally occurring processes; a firm stand by the parent is necessary, as by the analyst, only when they do not occur naturally. Consider weaning; it was in re-reading Winnicott's (1953) "Transitional object" paper that I was struck by the phrase already quoted at the beginning, because I feel it expresses just what I am trying to get at: "the mere termination of breast-feeding is not a weaning". This comes at the end of a paragraph where Winnicott is talking about "illusionment and disillusionment at the breast", where he says,

> the mother's main task . . . is disillusionment. This is preliminary to the task of weaning, and it also continues as one of the tasks of parents and educators . . . If things go well, in this gradual disillusionment process, the stage is set for the frustrations that we gather together under the word weaning . . . If illusion–disillusionment has gone astray the infant cannot attain to so normal a thing as weaning, nor to a reaction to weaning, and it is then absurd to refer to weaning at all. The mere termination of breastfeeding is not a weaning. [p. 13]

Termination criteria

I want to say something about criteria for termination, but not a great deal, because it is not the main issue I wish to discuss, though

I want to convey a flavour from the literature. In 1949, a symposium was held in the British Psychoanalytical Society on Criteria for Termination of Analysis, and there were one or two other articles round the world that were all gathered up into the 1950 volume of the *International Journal of Psychoanalysis*. Further useful reviews are in Firestein (1974, 1978), three Panels (1963, 1969, 1975) reported in the *Journal of the American Psychoanalytic Association*, and in the 1982 volume of *Psychoanalytic Inquiry*.

Balint (1950a) quotes Freud's early criteria for termination as: overcoming the patient's resistance; the removal of infantile amnesia; making the unconscious conscious (which Freud later, after 1923, rewrote as "Where id was there ego shall be"). Then, Balint points out, later developments were towards character analysis, and the analysis of object relations as they are revealed in the transference. In the second paper of Balint's (1950b), he classifies the criteria under three headings (but I think they are really two), that is, the achievement of genital primacy, which is a more complicated notion than mere genital potency, being a combination of genital satisfaction and pregenital tenderness; and the second one being the strengthening of the ego to cope with both pain and pleasure. Freud himself is usually quoted as saying mental health consists of the capacity to find satisfaction in love and work—I always think play should be added to that, so that we should say health consists of the capacity for love, work, and play. Firestein (1974) suggests that the origin of Freud's familiar maxim for assessing mental health comes from a statement in the *Introductory Lectures* referring to health in terms of "whether the subject is left with a sufficient amount of capacity for enjoyment and of efficiency" (Freud, 1916–1917, p. 457).

Ernest Jones (1936) listed several criteria: an increasing strength, confidence and well-being; a capacity for enjoyment and happiness; strengthening of the ego; a more tolerant superego; unconscious affects being allowed into consciousness, which should be tested in the sexual sphere (he says "if one cannot love then life loses much of its meaning"); also an increased capacity to deal with aggression; and he also mentioned symptomatic improvement. It is unfashionable in some circles to mention symptomatic improvement as a criterion, but Freud himself does, and Ernest Jones says, "it is possible to err in the opposite direction and to dismiss the importance of symptoms in a too cavalier fashion" (p. 380).

Sandor Lorand (1946) talks about an increased ability to find satisfaction in work; becoming more socially outgoing; finding more enjoyment, including sexual adjustment; that the repressed roots of neurosis should be revealed; unconscious impulses demonstrated; conflicts between superego, ego, and id eliminated; a strengthening of the ego; an increased tolerance of the superego. By the 1949 Symposium, Melanie Klein (1950) was able to refer to the "well-known criteria for termination", by which she apparently means a capacity for potency and heterosexuality; a capacity for love, object relations, and work; increased ego strength, and stability. And, in addition, she adds her own criteria: a diminution of persecutory and depressive anxieties; an analysis of both positive and negative aspects of the transference; and an analysis of mourning towards the end of therapy. Rickman (1950) listed six criteria (these become increasingly familiar): the removal of infantile amnesia; the capacity for heterosexual satisfaction; the capacity to tolerate frustration; the capacity for work, and, he adds, interestingly, to endure unemployment; a capacity to tolerate aggression in self and others; and a capacity to mourn.

I have attempted a summary of these criteria in two parts. First of all, these criteria of removing infantile amnesia; overcoming resistances; making the unconscious conscious, or "where id was there ego shall be". These all seem to me to be something to do with a diminution of defences, a diminution of inner splits or dissociations within the psyche. As Rycroft (1962) said, "In all forms of mental ill-health, however, dissociation occurs and the specific characteristics of both types of mental functioning [conscious and unconscious] become observable" (p. 388). So, we are dealing with healing of splits or inner dissociations. Those were some of the earlier criteria, and if we try to summarize the others together, many authors are talking about an increased capacity for heterosexual satisfaction; for work and unemployment; increased capacity for enjoyment, play, and relationships; increased tolerance of aggression, both in self and others; an increased capacity to cope with pain, pleasure, aggression, and sexuality; and for mourning. Now, all those could be simply listed under increased ego strength, which, along with a more tolerant superego, allows freer expression of feelings and drives.

So again, in perhaps a gross over-simplification, could we say that the criteria for termination come down to: increased ego strengths and a diminution of inner defences or inner dissociative processes? Rycroft (1962), further on in that same paper, says,

> If the hypothesis presented here is correct, the aim of psychoanalytical treatment is not primarily to make the unconscious conscious, nor to widen or strengthen the ego, but to re-establish the connexion between dissociated psychic functions, so that the patient ceases to feel that there is an inherent antagonism between his imaginative and adaptive capacities. [p. 393]

And he then goes on to quote E. M. Forster (1910):

> Only connect the prose and the passion . . . and both will be exalted, and human love will be seen at its height. Live in fragments no longer. Only connect, and the beast and the monk, robbed of the isolation that is life to either, will die. [Chapter 12]

So, although the above summary would be our rather formal criteria for termination, I think we could not do much better than simply quote E. M. Forster, "Only connect". Rycroft (1985) re-stated much the same later,

> psychoanalytical treatment is not so much a matter of making the unconscious conscious, or of widening and strengthening the ego, as of providing a setting in which healing can occur and connections with previously repressed, split-off and lost aspects of the self can be re-established. [p. 123]

There has been a general trend away from the earlier more ideal and formal criteria towards more realistic goals. These may be expressed in various developmental terms, for example, moving from the paranoid–schizoid to the depressive position, or by others in terms of facilitating emotional growth, or restoring the "developmental dialogue" (Erikson, 1980).

Gaskill (1980) underscores this "trend towards more modest expectations" and re-echoes an interesting theme developed by Stein (Panel, 1963), who traced the evolution of the novel in the late eighteenth and nineteenth centuries from plots with fairy-tale endings, through Dickens to Proust, towards a greater concern with character. The changing goals of analysis, he suggests, have paralleled the evolution of the novel from earlier concerns with happy endings in heterosexual potency, towards the more complex development of characters.

Many authors (Firestein, 1978; Novick, 1982; Siegel, 1982; Ticho, 1972) have emphasized a trend towards recognizing the capacity for self-analysis as a principal criterion for termination. Firestein (1982) makes a further point about over-emphasizing formal criteria. He attempted a replication of Glover's (1955) earlier questionnaire survey of members of the British Psychoanalytical Society, who acknowledged that their termination criteria were essentially intuitive. In answer to the question, "Of the numerous criteria discussed in the literature on termination of psychoanalysis, which have you found to be the most useful in arriving at the decision to terminate?", Firestein observes:

> Although in the literature criteria are often framed in the language of metapsychology, such language was not prominent at all in the responses of my interviewees. Their usage was decidedly clinical— a clear reflection of their translation of metapsychological constructs into the language of observables. [*ibid.*, p. 485]

He later concludes:

> Statements on termination couched in metapsychological language have an elegance that contrasts sharply to the degree of approximation involved in our efforts to apply guidelines to the actual clinical situations with which we labour. [*ibid.*, p. 495]

Ticho (1972) makes the important distinction between life goals and treatment goals. His attention was first drawn to the importance of the difference as a member of the Psychotherapy Research Project of the Menninger Foundation. Many analysts were anxious about their work being studied, which Ticho dubbed "research anxiety", often due, he felt, to the analyst's unconscious confusion between treatment goals and life goals. He quotes Winnicott:

> You may cure your patient and not know what it is that makes him or her go on living. It is of first importance for us to acknowledge openly that absence of psychoneurotic illness may be health, but it is not life. [1967b, p. 100]

Termination, possible or impossible?

Now, can analysis be ended satisfactorily or not? This problem is the basis of Freud's (1937c) "Analysis terminable and interminable". He asks, "Is there such a thing as a natural end to an analysis?" (p. 219). He gives his two conditions for ending—when there is no longer suffering from symptoms, and when the repressed is made conscious and internal resistances conquered. We have already considered these points. Note that he puts symptoms first; he does not scorn symptomatic improvement. He then talks of a more ambitious ending, when there is nothing more to achieve, but realizes that a balance has to be struck between constitutional factors, such as strength of instinct, and traumatic factors. "Only when a case is predominantly traumatic . . . only in such cases can one speak of an analysis having been definitely ended" (ibid., p. 220). And he points out that training analyses have to be longer, but may still be incomplete. He is here hinting at the difficulties he himself experienced with Ferenczi, due to the unresolved hostile feelings from Ferenczi towards himself. He then goes on to say, "Every analyst should periodically—at intervals of five years or so—submit himself to analysis once more" (ibid., p. 249). Elsewhere, he makes the modest claim, which I think is worth remembering, since some people (e.g., Grinberg, 1980) think of analysis as something very special and unique, that "what analysis achieves for neurotics is nothing other than what normal people bring about for themselves without its help" Freud, 1937c, p. 225), and further on Freud says, "The business of the analysis is to secure the best possible psychological conditions for the functions of the ego; with that it has discharged its task" (ibid., p. 250).

Buxbaum (1950) agreed with Freud that it is only in traumatic cases that termination really occurs so easily, and that character neuroses often prove interminable. Zetzel (Panel, 1969) is reported as saying,

In the optimal group of patients, in whom the major conflicts are derived from an unresolved oedipal situation, she believes the transference neurosis can be resolved. In her practice, she added significantly, very few patients could be classified in this most favorable group. More frequently one finds that defences and other

influences have been initiated during the preoedipal dyadic relationship, and the analyst is then obliged to accept limitations to the
degree of resolution of the transference neurosis. [p. 229]

Klauber (1981) in a paper on "Analyses that cannot be terminated", writes about two cases with whom he had extreme difficulty in ending. They both showed considerable early maternal
deprivation, and he felt they were much more in the nature of
borderline cases than the more ordinary neurotic case, which could
be satisfactorily terminated. Freud's view—shared by others—that
only traumatic cases are really successful seems to link with
Malan's (1963) recommendations in brief focal psychotherapy: that
there is a need for a focus, which works out best where there is a
conflict at a neurotic Oedipal level. Brief focal psychotherapy is
much less relevant or appropriate where there are more difficult,
borderline, or pre-Oedipal problems.

Technique, changed or unchanging?

An issue much discussed in the literature (Firestein, 1974, 1978,
1982; Panel, 1969, 1975) is whether or not there should be any
change in technique towards the end of analysis or psychotherapy.
Should one continue five times, or however many times it is, until
the end, or should the frequency be decreased? Should there be
contact with the analyst afterwards? Should there be follow-up
visits? I remember, in a seminar on Termination in London, it was
stated that analysis took place five times a week, and it continued
five times a week until the end. If more analysis was needed, that
should also be five times a week. I felt that was a rather inflexible
position, particularly since I had begun my own analysis three
times a week, increasing it to five times a week before the period of
my training and beyond, and then diminishing it again finally. So
that kind of development and *crescendo–diminuendo* seems much
more relevant to me.

However, opinions differ about this. Most of Firestein's (1982)
respondents to his questionnaire made no changes. Dewald (1982)
is also not in favour of changes which he considers imply a failure of the analytic situation. Buxbaum (1950) spoke in favour of

diminishing frequency towards the end of analysis, but, in the 1969 Panel, analysts are reported as having very varying views. Greenson (Panel, 1975) is reported as saying that he invites patients to sit up and face him in the last two weeks of analysis, and also to return at monthly intervals for a few months afterwards. Several other authors leave it open for the patient to return. Buxbaum (1950) used the phrase "to keep the door open for a patient to return for a visit", so that it becomes much more like a leaving home. Zetzel (Panel, 1969) says she

> regards no analysis as successfully terminated unless the patient feels free to return in case of further troubles. This is especially true with regard to candidates, unless the latter feel free to disagree with her in a professional situation; "The candidate should not feel that he has to maintain an idealised or totally positive identification". [p. 229]

Termination for analysts?

If it is maintained that termination is the right phrase, and that ending should be final, complete, and abrupt, then are we not asking patients to face something that we as analysts may never, or seldom, have to face? After qualification, a new analyst may continue to meet their analyst at professional meetings, may collaborate professionally in teaching, committee work, and so forth, or may become closely identified as one of the main heirs and disciples of their analyst. Of course, there are risks of idealization here—especially in longer analyses—and there may be a suppression of negative feelings. The analysand may alternatively become engaged in the opposite, and react against everything their analyst stands for if there is an unanalysed idealization which then collapses.

It has often struck me, in the British Psychoanalytical Society, how we pay particular attention to the death of member analysts—which is a very appropriate and agreeable custom. When an analyst dies, who is known to others, one or more people make obituary remarks at our next scientific meeting. These are often very personal memoirs. Then we also later on have more formal memorial meetings, for a better known analyst, for instance as we did for Anna Freud a few years ago. But I have often wondered if this attention given to the death of colleagues is not an important further step in the termination of many analysts' analyses. Limentani (1982) in his paper on "unexpected termination", writes,

> ... Nor does the end of a training analysis help, because even when an identification with the analyst has been circumvented, there still remains an identification with his or her analysing functions. Moreover, the possibility of further contacts is always there. The eventual death of the analyst will at times be "unexpected" ... simply because there has not been an actual and final termination as we understand it to take place in all other therapeutic relationships. [p. 439]

Reich (1950) compares termination and mourning (to which I return) and suggests that:

> as in mourning a spontaneous recovery takes place, we might say a recovery from the abnormal situation of analysis. With students who have the occasion to meet their analyst professionally after termination of analysis this process progresses faster. They have the opportunity to see their analysts in the frame of reality, and the magic omnipotent features of the relationship collapse more readily under these conditions and may be replaced by a mature friendship or a working relationship. The final solution of these last traces of transference can be considered as a final growing up of the patient. [p. 183]

Buxbaum (1950), whom I have already quoted as in favour of diminishing the frequency of sessions towards the end, and allowing patients to return, points out that, for some patients, parting means a death of the analyst, especially where there have been deaths in reality before. She goes on,

> there are other cases, too, and for other reasons, where some relationship with the patient has to be continued after the end of analysis. In working with candidates in training or in doing a second analysis with colleagues, contacts after the end of the analysis are usual ... I consider it a sign of successful analysis if the former patient feels at ease and can "take or leave" the analyst. But it seems

to me, particularly in a small group with frequent contacts, that it takes about a year after the end of the analysis for the patient to reach a certain equilibrium with the analyst. [*ibid.*, p. 189]

Note that she says "about a year"—which is often a socially agreed mourning period. Milner (1950) put this more strongly, saying that analysts bypass the experience patients have to go through. And, incidentally, she skilfully avoids the use of the word "termination" at all in her paper, which is called "A note on the ending of analysis". She is the only author I have come across who manages to avoid the use of the word "termination". She says,

Although there is perhaps no such thing as a completed analysis, most patients do, sooner or later, stop coming to analysis. Perhaps we, as analysts, are handicapped in knowing all about what ending feels like, for by the mere fact of becoming analysts we have succeeded in bypassing an experience which our patients have to go through. We have chosen to identify ourselves with our analyst's profession and to act out that identification—a thing which our patients on the whole are not able to do. [*ibid.*, p. 191]

Termination and mourning

I have already compared the ending of analysis with mourning, and this is linked with the whole complex phenomenon of internalization of lost objects in mourning. This was not yet fully worked out by Freud (1917b) when he wrote "Mourning and melancholia". He did not yet see internalization as part of normal mourning, because, in 1917, a theory of internal objects and internal object-relationships was only just beginning. It becomes more clear after 1923, and I have pointed out before (Pedder, 1982) how a process similar to that of internalization in mourning is seen not only in phases of child-hood development, but also in the satisfactory progress and termi-nation of psychotherapy and analysis, or any form of education or training. Ferenczi (1927) was one of the first to compare termination with mourning, for a lost source of gratification, when he wrote, "The renunciation of analysis is thus the final winding up of the infantile situation of frustration which lay at the basis of symptom-formation" (p. 85).

Reich (1950) quotes a very clear comparison of the ending of analysis with mourning from a patient who came to her for a second training analysis, several years after the first analysis with another analyst: His description of his reaction to the termination of his first analysis was quite revealing:

> I felt as if I was suddenly left alone in the world. It was like the feel-ing that I had after the death of my mother . . . I tried with effort to find somebody to love, something to be interested in. For months I longed for the analyst and wished to tell him about whatever happened to me. Then slowly, without noticing how it happened, I forgot about him. About two years later, I happened to meet him at a party and thought he was just a nice elderly gentleman and in no way interesting. [p. 182]

Balint (1950b) also, in describing his concept of new beginning, which he felt occurred towards the end of a successful analysis, writes how

> the general atmosphere is of taking leave for ever of something very dear, very precious—with all the corresponding grief and mourning—but this sincere and deeply felt grief is mitigated by the feeling of security, originating from the newly-won possibilities for real happiness. Usually the patient leaves after the last session happy but with tears in his eyes and—I think I may admit—the analyst is in a very similar mood. [p. 197]

Though he does go on to say that this rather rosy ending occurs only in about two out of ten cases.

DeBell (Panel, 1975) in a paper on "Termination, technique and mourning the analyst as an object", discussed the problem of mourning the analyst as a real person, which include: in the termi-nation phase, the mourning work of giving up the analyst as real object, which the analyst has become during the course of the analysis. In De Bell's opinion, giving up the analyst as a real object cannot be solved by analysis; this loss cannot be analysed, it can only be borne. Mourning is not necessarily prominent or overt, and is only resolved later by internalization (*ibid.*, p. 169). So, mourning and internalization are recognized as closely linked phenomena in termination, as in other developmental stages.

Grinberg (1980) takes up this issue of internalization and its relationship to termination:

> I believe that analysis does not terminate with the separation of the analyst and the analysand. The only thing which ends is the relationship between them, giving way to a new phase of continuation of the process through self-analysis. . . . In other words, the psychoanalytic relationship is terminated, or is about to end, when the psychoanalytic process has been internalised by the analysand. [*ibid.*, p. 27]

This touches on one of the difficulties with the word termination. It is a portmanteau term which refers to several different processes, but with at least two distinct trends. These are, on the one hand, the actual cessation of visits to the analyst (though even this may be blurred by subsequent meetings); and, on the other hand, a continuation of the now-internalized analytic process. Loewald (1962) links the themes of internalization and mourning in his paper entitled "Internalisation, separation, mourning and the superego". He likens ending to a long-drawn-out leave-taking:

> The relinquishment of external objects and their internalization involves a process of separation, of loss and restitution in many ways similar to mourning . . . In fact, the end-phase of an analysis may be described as a long-drawn-out leave-taking . . . [p. 484]

Patients at the termination of treatment frequently express a feeling of mutual abandonment, which, if analysed, becomes the pathway to the relinquishment of the analyst as an external object and to the internalization of the relationship. This is similar to the experience of emancipation in adolescence, which repeats the Oedipal struggle on a higher level (*ibid.*, p. 495).

Developmental stages

We have already seen how Loewald has compared the mourning and separation of termination with similar phenomena occurring at earlier developmental stages, such as the resolution of the Oedipal conflict and of adolescence. Stock (Panel, 1969) reviewed descriptions of what is involved in the resolution of transference neurosis.

> This process . . . is often accompanied by feelings of rage and of
> disillusionment with the analysis . . . Several analysts stressed the
> resemblance between this process and the process of individuation
> which is resumed in the course of normal adolescence. [*ibid.*, p. 224]

And in the discussion there were numerous references by other
speakers to the analytic termination process as parallel to the
adolescent maturational process. Dewald (1982), among others,
compares "the termination of therapy and the process of emancipation during adolescence". Parents (and therapists) must accept
they have done the best they can, and it is now out of their hands.

Silverman (1971), in a paper with an intriguing title containing
the phrase "Termination of analysis: graduation–initiation rite",
wrote,

> After nearly four years of analysis, I accepted the patient's request
> for a specific date to terminate . . . After agreeing on an actual date
> for termination of his analysis, the patient behaved as one under-
> going the painful ordeal of a puberty rite or of graduation–initia-
> tion ceremonies. [*ibid.*, p. 290]

Silverman's patient had actually spent the same number of years in
analysis as he had done at college. It is not uncommon, if not ideal,
for patients to decide to terminate at the moment of finishing a
course. This patient of Silverman's referred to the last day of his
analysis as his Graduation Day, and also as his Birthday. In this
case, the idea of the word "Graduation" seems to be more that of
the patient than the analyst. But it is similar to the expression used
by patients in a slow open psychotherapy group that I run at the
Maudsley Hospital, where patients may enter the group and
remain there for two or three years before leaving. And they often
refer to each other's appropriate and satisfactory leaving as a
Graduation. I think it is interesting that we often think of psychotherapy or analysis maybe lasting three or four years, the period of
a course at a university, the period that any substantial personality
development or change takes. So the idea of Graduation perhaps is
one of the better phrases I can think of so far. For some, it may have
too academic a connotation, though essentially it means to take a
step. [A further disadvantage is that for some people graduation

may be synonomous with qualification as an analyst (see IPA Monograph No. 5—*The Termination of the Training Analysis*).]

Finally, Sylvia Payne (1950) compares the ending of analysis with many different developmental stages, when she says,

> I have found the end compared with the anxieties of growing up, leaving school, leaving the university, rebirth, weaning, the end of mourning, all being critical times involving a reorganization of ego and libidinal interests. [*ibid.*, p. 205]

Disillusionment

I have already referred to the discussion in the 1969 Panel, which compared disillusionment with analysis to the process of individuation which is resumed in the course of normal adolescence. This leads back to the same process of disillusionment associated with earlier developmental phases, and particularly that of weaning. Winnicott (1953) emphasized how gradual disillusionment is a necessary part of every infant's development, especially in weaning, where the illusion of omnipotent control of the breast has to give way to disillusionment. And he emphasized it occurs again in adolescents, who have not yet settled down into disillusionment but are free to be idealists, not yet having to accept adult responsibilities.

Although the theme of disillusionment recurs throughout Winnicott's writings, it cannot be familiar enough, since Novick (1982) can write,

> Seldom mentioned in the literature is the necessity for disillusionment in order to begin the process of giving up and mourning the omnipotent mother–child dyad. To a certain extent, the analyst must be experienced as a failure for the patient to respond fully to the treatment as a success. [p. 362]

Gradual disillusionment is a necessary part of every infant's development. A similar process of disillusionment happens to all of us on waking from a dream, or to the patient recovering from the nightmare of a psychotic breakdown. It is an essential part of the ending of any successful psychoanalytic psychotherapy. And, of course, it happens when the house lights go up at the end of a play (Pedder, 1977), as Prospero says, towards the end of *The Tempest*:

> Our revels now are ended. These our actors,
> As I foretold you, were all spirits, and
> Are melted into air, into thin air . . .

But what happens, after the curtain descends? I agree with the many analysts who say we cannot know the outcome of psychotherapy or analysis until long after its ending. Marion Milner's (1950) patient did not even begin to lose her major symptom of headaches until after the analysis ended. Klauber (1981) says, in the introduction to *Difficulties in the Analytic Encounter*,

> I try to base my own technique on one cardinal assumption. This is that psychoanalysis is a long process in which what happens after the patient has left the psychoanalyst's consulting room for the last time is more important than what happens during the analysis. [p. xvi]

So, who knows what the outcome of analysis, or the outcome of any psychotherapy training or course, will be? What will be internalized when it ends?

I began with Winnicott and end with a quote from T. S. Eliot, which, incidentally (C. Winnicott, 1978), was included by Winnicott on the inside flap of the notebook of his unfinished autobiography: "What we call the beginning is often the end. And to make an end is to make a beginning. The end is where we start from . . ." (Eliot, 1943, *Little Gidding*).

Commentary (GW) on Chapter Six: Reflections on the theory and practice of supervision

Here, Pedder talks about the dual function of supervision, where sometimes supervision can feel more like therapy and therapy can feel more like supervision. He offers an accessible account of supervision with lively metaphors taken from gardening, including potting and pruning among the gamut of supervisory activities, bringing alive the process of supervision with some straightforward advice about the challenges that face the clinical supervisor. The chapter has an advisory tone, combined with a sort of tendermindedness (see Chapter Seven, where Pedder uses the term), and I think the chapter offers a good reflection of some of the essences of Pedder's supervisory style in practice.

My experience as one of his many supervisees was that he would, on occasions, offer up straightforward counsel about things I might do or say (potting an idea). At other times he would tell me what he would do or say in certain situations, especially, I think, when my interventions might have been misplaced (this was the pruning, perhaps). He was especially steadying and nurturing following the death of one my colleagues and then, shortly afterwards, a patient I had been working with. His straightforward counsel at this time was memorable; I remember he told me that sometimes after a trauma, "the best one can do is hold on to one's chair". There are times when words fail.

At first I found his direct style unexpected, but then refreshing and helpful. A new therapist's self discovery ought to be balanced by the wisdom of ages and others, though there was never any impression that Pedder's suggestions were dictates. There were occasions he would tell me that he did not understand what I meant. And I remember one occasion when he wrote some feedback on an essay I was writing, which read, "I don't understand this, maybe I'm not supposed to". It felt a bit like what I think Winnicott meant when he said misunderstanding was normalizing, it meant we lived in the real world. As a consequence, I always felt accepted in supervision, a sense of quiet being-with. This is not to say that supervision was without conflict. For instance, during a training group I ran during the First Gulf War, I was sure that my approach needed to be modified. "Peace-time" receded and I felt I ought to take this into account as the external politic was riling; it seemed my primary attention to my patients' formative experiences needed to be reconsidered in light of the external crisis. The social dislocation of the patients, at least for the time being, seemed better understood in reverse. That is to say, what might be understood without, might have helped the patients make sense of within. The outside world did indeed seem to be pressing in. One of my group sessions took place on the day that Downing Street was hit in a mortar attack. That afternoon there were sirens on Denmark Hill outside the Maudsley Hospital psychotherapy department; it was pandemonium, and I was sure that in a time of war, therapy must be different. Pedder told me that he thought that it should be treatment as usual and that there was "no such thing as peace time". It is worth noting that, in this chapter, he suggests a war and peace continuum, so the idea of "no such thing as peace time" might be taken as absolute, a bit like Winnicott's "no such thing as a baby". In relation to the idea that therapy should continue as usual during a time of war, Pedder's stoical rejoinder does have echoes of the occasions during the "controversial discussions" at the Institute of Psychoanalysis in London during the Second World War, where debates continued unabated in spite of the circumstances outside. Famously, one evening the argument had been so fierce that no one had noticed the bombing going on outside, until a young Donald

Winnicott pointed out that there was indeed an air-raid going on. The assorted gathering did not head for the nearest shelter, but instead took their chairs down to the basement, where the debate continued. There is something about this muffled attitude which makes psychoanalysis simultaneously abiding and resolute, but also remote and insulated.

On a lighter note, Pedder does talk in this chapter about supervision as play. I am in no doubt that he allowed me to play with many ideas, but the atmosphere was always business-like, and even if I had a sense of his tendermindedness, his approach was always cool and lofty. Pedder is keen to convey a sense that NHS psychoanalytic therapy is, at best, an active approach, task orientated with a view to safety, and that it needs to be a moving and active engagement rather than a pedestrian one. I did have a point of disagreement with him in regard to the "activity" of a couple of my male patients, who went through a phase of falling asleep in sessions (individual and group). I thought the falling asleep might be a marker for progress, in so far as the patient might have felt safe enough to fall asleep. Pedder thought the sleeping ought to be discouraged, and that it was more likely to be a defence against contact, and not a willing submission to relaxation. I disagreed at the time, but, with hindsight, I now concur. Therapy needs to be active, not in the Ferenczian sense, but, rather, where awakeness primes the best use of time.

I would just add one more comment of appreciation about Pedder's support, especially when I would take him drafts of my earlier attempts at writing about my clinical work. His diligence in reading my essays and drafts of inchoate papers was generous, to say the least. He would return my manuscripts promptly, and always with detailed and copious red pen marks. He would suggest terms I could use, sometimes more simple than those I was using. I recall him suggesting that I should use the Anglo-Saxon equivalent to one of my turns of phrase, which might seem a surprise from a pro-European. When my colleague Sally Hardy saw one of his edits, she coined the term "Pedderism" to denote an exemplar of fine-grain mentoring. As I began to read his writings beyond his *Introduction to Psychotherapy*, I saw how an academic account of therapy should be rendered: clear, precise, accurate, and engaging. It is this attitude that we see here in this chapter. A range of supervisory responsibilities and hats, from educative to pastoral, from advisory to therapeutic, they are described with clear markers for the potentials and pitfalls of good supervision. To my mind, the framework for supervision here easily stretches across a range of caring professions, from psychotherapists and counsellors, to nurses, psychiatrists, social workers, and psychologists. In the chapter, Pedder also refers in some detail to Balint's work with general practitioners (GPs) and notes how Balint would require the GPs, usually familiar with the discipline of note-taking, to endure the experience of speaking without notes when presenting a case to the group. We might think of the supervisory atmosphere outlined by Pedder as one of disciplined spontaneity. It is not unstructured in the sense that psychodynamic supervision is sometimes portrayed; rather, Pedder outlines a highly regarded set of principles which might be deployed to foster the most conducive and creative supervisory milieu where the quality of clinical practice can be enhanced through meaningful shared reflection between supervisor and supervisee.

Reflections on the theory and practice of supervision

Education, supervision, therapy

I t is an old aphorism, often quoted (e.g., Solnit, 1970), that supervision is "more than education and less than psychotherapy". Although it is an old cliché, I think it offers a valuable dimension along which we can begin to consider the whole issue of supervision. Yet, this immediately poses the question: to what extent is it "more than education" and "less than psychotherapy"? And that poses further questions, such as what kind of education is supervision more than, and what form of psychotherapy is it less than? For education itself may vary along a whole continuum as well, from a very didactic form of teaching, or indoctrination, to what I would call proper education, leading people out, or drawing people out, which, after all, must be very much like what we imagine we are doing in exploratory psychotherapy.

Psychotherapy, too, can obviously vary from very directive forms to the most non-directive forms. So, if supervision is to be pitched somewhere along a spectrum between education and psychotherapy, then how far from either end should it be? Perhaps this depends on the level of development of the trainee. Just as with psychotherapy itself, the level of psychotherapy will vary with the developmental level of the patient. A more disturbed patient may need more directive support; a healthier patient needs much less. Similarly, an infant needs firm support; an adolescent must begin to go his own way.

Thinking of such developmental lines recalls Freud's (1937c) three impossible tasks: analysis, education, and government. A common factor might be the need to reconcile the irreconcilable, and each may vary in style from directive to non-directive. Government may need to be more dictatorial in time of war or crisis, more non-directive and permissive in peace. Schlessinger (1966) cites Rosenbaum as suggesting

> the initial assignment of kindly supervisors to his residents to serve as proper models and provide some support during the early anxieties about doing therapy, with subsequent exposure to more demanding supervisors at a later point in the residency.

Supervisor as jug, potter, or gardener

Fleming (1967) talks of three models of both teaching and supervision: the jug, potter, and gardener models. The jug model, where information is merely poured into a passive recipient; the potter model, where the potter starts with a lump of clay and fashions it into something after his own image; the gardener model, which is the one I much prefer, where you provide the soil, do a bit of pruning, tend the plant, do some watering, put it in the right degree of light, and trust in its own innate processes of growth and development. You take a supervisee from where he is, do some pruning, and hope he will develop his own style. And that very much reflects my own view of what psychotherapy or supervision is about: it is about promoting growth in people.

We have to take trainees from where they are—most have had considerable background experience of dealing with people in a therapeutic role, whether as doctor, psychologist, social worker, or nurse. They are not empty vessels into whom we pour from a jug, nor inert lumps of clay to be fashioned after our own image. We are facilitators, gardeners, accepting the plants that spring up in our gardens and doing what we can by pruning.

This model of pruning was suggested in Michael and Enid Balint's (1961) book *Psychotherapeutic Techniques in Medicine*. Actually, they first use this metaphor in describing the function of the doctor (particularly a general practitioner) in educating a patient about his illness:

> that aspect of the doctor's teaching function which may be called the shaping of the patient's illness. This happens by an interaction that has been described elsewhere as "the patient's offers" of illnesses and "the doctor's responses" to them. Using a simile from gardening, one could say that the patient grows an illness and it is the doctor who trains it by pruning some symptoms, allowing others to go on growing while forcing yet others to take a direction that he prescribes to them. Of course, the doctor cannot do everything, his powers are as limited as the gardener's . . . [*ibid.*, p. 105]

However, I think it is also a very good metaphor that psychotherapy, and supervision too, are like pruning.

Supervision and psychotherapy as play

Supervision also parallels psychotherapy to the extent that it creates a regular space, a regular time and place, for taking a second look, a re-search, reflecting on what has happened in the psychotherapy session between patient and therapist. This concept of the regular time and space needed for supervision recalls Winnicott's idea of a potential play space and suggests a parallel between the idea of psychotherapy as play and that of supervision as playing with ideas. Winnicott (1971) wrote "Psychotherapy takes place in the overlap of two areas of playing, that of the patient and that of the therapist. Psychotherapy has to do with two people playing together". Perhaps we could paraphrase that and say supervision takes place in the overlap of two areas of playing, that of the therapist and that of the supervisor. Michael Balint also noted a "similarity between Winnicott's diagnostic therapeutic interviews and our techniques" (in Balint & Norell, 1973).

In the very act of writing notes on a case for supervision, one is reflecting on it and already entering into that process, or in the act of re-reading the notes in supervision, or in responding in supervision to notes previously made, ideas occur and you wonder (I did as a supervisee) why you did not think of them at the time. Analysts of all levels of experience may find they learn something new by reporting on a case. Even an analyst as experienced as Greenson (1967) has found this:

> Let me illustrate: I have been working for many years with a patient and in my considered judgement things are going slowly but well. I would have stated that I like the patient and am satisfied with our work. Yet, one day when I meet the analyst who referred her to me, in response to his question about how she was doing, I found myself saying, "Well, you know she is a Qvetsch". (Qvetsch is a Yiddish word meaning a chronic "groaner" or complainer.) I am surprised at my remark, but later realise: (a) it was accurate; (b) I had not consciously realised it before; (c) I was unconsciously protecting the patient from my discontent with her. After this conversation I began to work on this problem both with her and within myself. [p. 70]

Internalization

When we finish our psychoanalytic or psychotherapy training, we all, we hope, internalize models of our own analysts, therapists, and supervisors, and this helps us to analyse our own hang-ups as well as the problems we have with our patients. Internalization is a complex psychological phenomenon, common to many processes of development and change. It recalls Freud's aphorism that "the character of the ego is the precipitate of abandoned object-cathexes" (Freud, 1923b), or, in other words, we build up our inner world of objects or images from internal representations of past important relationships.

Normal grief and mourning must be one of the best known examples of internalization of the lost object (Pedder, 1982). If all goes well, and especially if a good prior relationship with the lost person was enjoyed, one is left with a good internal object, with memories and experiences of the lost person which are sustaining. A process similar to that of internalization in mourning is seen not only in phases of childhood development, but also in the satisfactory progress and termination (or "graduation", as discussed in the previous chapter) of psychotherapy and psychoanalysis, or any form of education or training, recalling again the common theme of Freud's three impossible tasks, at least two of which require the internalization of some self-sustaining agency.

It also echoes Winnicott's (1958) view that "the capacity to be alone is based on the experience of being alone in the presence of someone (i.e. originally mother), and that without a sufficiency of this experience the capacity to be alone cannot develop" (p. 33). Might we not paraphrase that and say that the capacity to work alone as a therapist is based on the experience of having been alone in the presence of someone (i.e., originally analyst and/or supervisor) and that without a sufficiency of this experience the capacity to work alone cannot develop? I certainly have internal conversations with past supervisors or with people whom I respect, and, when in difficulties with patients, I may hold such internal conversations with myself. I report on a case to an imaginary supervisor, and in the very act of that kind of internal dialogue, which takes place externally in supervision, new things may emerge, as occurred in the example already quoted above from Greenson (1967).

Records

That leads straight into the issue of notes and records of sessions, and I am not going to say much about this. We have passionate advocates for all sorts of different ways of recording sessions, from detailed written records, audio-tapes or video-tapes, to no records at all, where a method of spontaneous reporting might be deployed. I am sure all these have something to offer, and they all lose something. Each may be useful or defensive in some ways. Tapes might apparently be the most accurate way of recording what happens in the session, certainly what has outwardly and apparently happened, but would say nothing about the inner life of the psychotherapist.

On the other hand, some people can hide behind detailed written records, even the most exhaustive kind, unless one pauses for the stage directions as well. Balint, in the GP seminars, would not allow any written records at all. He required people to speak spontaneously of what they remembered and what they felt about the patient, without written records.

The structure of supervision

I should like to consider further some of these similarities and differences between psychotherapy and supervision, and the contrasts I have found in supervision of individual psychotherapy, especially between supervising people individually, one to one, and supervising people in a group. In the Psychotherapy Unit at the Maudsley, we are used to supervising trainee psychiatrists who come to the Unit for nine months as part of their three-year general psychiatry training, and we do that individually. We are also used to supervising, as many others are, small groups of trainees (mostly psychiatrists, but also other disciplines) who are not working on the Unit but who are following the guidelines of the Royal College of Psychiatrists (1971) and are taking on one or two cases for individual psychotherapy under supervision for maybe a year or two throughout their general psychiatry training.

Consider some of the differences and problems that arise in these two different settings: how much the situation should be structured or not; and what happens as a consequence. Much of the literature is from America, or from a psychoanalytic tradition of supervision, and assumes that many of the trainees are also in therapy, which they may or may not be in the UK. Several papers (e.g., Frijling-Schreuder, 1970; Lebovici, 1970) emphasize the difficulties that may arise when transference problems occur in psychotherapy supervision with the supervisor. I know it happens, because in my own psychoanalytic training I had a male analyst and two female supervisors, and I am well aware that some aspects of more maternal, feminine transferences got split off on to my female supervisors. These displaced transferences are more likely to occur where the sex of the analyst is opposite to the sex of the supervisor. I have known that occur with supervisees who have had female analysts, and some aspects of what I think were father transferences were being split off and re-enacted towards me as supervisor.

Now, we know that transference is increased whenever regression takes place, that it is accentuated in classical analysis, using the couch, or when people are acutely ill or anxious. These are the kinds of situation that promote transference phenomena. Solnit (1970) agreed with Frijling-Schreuder (1970), at the Rome Pre-Congress Conference on training, that one should not encourage regression by the student in supervision. Well, that sounds very sensible, but how do you do that, how do you actually make sure that such things never occur in individual supervision? I think one way we do it is by having group supervisions, because it does not happen then to the same extent. There is less tendency to regress in a group. It is much easier for a group to remain task-orientated, on the job of sorting out the individual therapist's cases, and personal issues arise much less.

Balint began his GP seminars by saying "Who's got a case?", and I expect that most of us begin group psychotherapy supervision seminars by saying something like "Who's going to speak first? Who is going to talk?" We do not say "How are you all feeling?" We do not promote any general discussion of issues outside the actual work in hand.

Not everyone agrees that there is always less tendency to regress in a group. Frijling-Schreuder (1970) writes,

> In group supervision anxiety may be diminished by knowing that the other students are in a similar position. In addition, group members may profit from each other's observations. In the psychiatric training of residents these group experiences may be of high value. However, in psychoanalytic training this procedure has great disadvantages because membership of a group inevitably leads to regressive processes. In particular, the primitive, archaic forms of rivalry over the leader and between group members are aroused. [p. 369]

In individual psychotherapy supervision, it seems to me that it is often very impersonal to start straight away to focus on work, as one might in a group. This may be a fault of mine, not to be structured enough in the individual situation, but if we are too structured it seems to me we ignore the tutorial and pastoral needs of the trainee therapist. It might be argued that these tutoring and supervising roles ought to be separated. Psychoanalytic training attempts to separate the roles by having a Progress Adviser as well as a supervisor and analyst, but I think a Progress Adviser is often a pretty remote figure, and may not often be seen.

However, for the registrars at the Maudsley, coming to the Psychotherapy Unit for nine months, the consultant/supervisor is partly tutor as well. And then, of course, we get into problems, because if we start supervisory sessions by saying, "How are things going?", which seems quite legitimate when a person is just starting, asking about general problems of arranging their schedule, finding enough patients, and so on, inevitably we open ourselves to all manner of problems. Somebody may have suffered a bereavement, somebody may be divorcing, having a baby; all kinds of things may be happening that they may want to talk about, and we get something that starts up much more like a therapy session. Obviously, that depends partly on whether the person at the time is in therapy himself or not.

So, it occurs to me that the amount of structure we put into the supervision will determine how much it is like therapy, or is not like therapy, and we avoid these problems to a large extent by supervising in groups, because in groups people are less likely to bring up personal issues. They might in moments of tremendous crisis, but on the whole they do not.

The influence of Michael Balint

I have mentioned Balint several times, and many will be familiar with the GP seminars that he started at the Tavistock Clinic. What may be less familiar is how that method arose out of the Hungarian psychoanalytic training situation. It is described in an appendix to *The Doctor, His Patient and the Illness* (Balint, 1957), where one of the appendices is on training and general practice. It is generally assumed in most formal psychotherapy training that the supervisor and the therapist are going to be different people, but it has not always been the case. Fordham (1978) emphasizes how, in the Jungian tradition, analyst and supervisor were often the same person. In the first place, it was Jung himself who took on both tasks. Perhaps the answer is that it is likely to happen where personnel are limited, when there simply are not enough people to split these tasks. That was the situation in Budapest, where there was Balint's analyst Ferenczi, Balint himself, his first wife, and one or two others, but there were so few you simply could not have had a wider system. So, the tradition was, rather than go to a separate supervisor, your first supervisor was your own analyst. As Balint puts it, on four days of the week you talked about yourself, and on the fifth you talked about your patient. Obviously, therefore, the patient was approached through the countertransference, through the trainee therapist's own feelings about the patient, entirely through free association, without the use of any notes; the patient, the analysand, lying on a couch, just free-associating as usual, but about his case. And, of course, I know from my own analysis, and particularly from continuing analysis while starting doing intense analytical and psychotherapeutic work, that in a few minutes I often got much more from discussing a problem via the countertransference with my analyst than I felt I would have got from much more lengthy discussions elsewhere.

When Michael and Enid Balint started training social workers first of all, in the Family Discussion Bureau at the Tavistock Clinic, it was this Hungarian system that they adopted, because these trainees, as they point out in the appendix (Balint, 1957), on the whole had not had their own personal therapy, so they had to find a way of getting at the trainees' own personal feelings, without slipping over too much into therapy. They did not allow notes; they encouraged free-floating discussion, which, of course, relies on the therapist's feelings about their clients, that is, their countertransference. And this is the method which he then adapted for GPs, and, when he retired from the Tavistock Clinic, which he took to University College Hospital (London), where he helped start the tradition of medical student psychotherapy. I think it is a model which has been very influential in British psychotherapy training. As Pines (1974) wrote,

> It is remarkable how many of the post-war innovations in psychotherapy training in this country are connected with the work of Michael Balint. Throughout his long and distinguished psychoanalytic career, he sowed the seeds of fruitful research. He formed the nucleus of a psychoanalytic training centre in Manchester; began the Tavistock general practitioner seminars; a short-term psychotherapy workshop staffed by psychoanalysts from the Cassel Hospital and Tavistock Clinic was the source of David Malan's monograph on brief psychotherapy; he started the Family Planning Association seminars in the treatment of psychosexual problems; he finally moved on to undergraduate teaching at University College Hospital. His work on the training seminar—"the Balint Seminar" has had a world-wide impact. [pp. 296–297]

Now, of course, many training schemes, in psychoanalysis or psychotherapy, have clinical seminars in addition to individual supervision, and these, too, are groups, but they may only meet for a limited number of occasions, whereas the ongoing psychotherapy supervision group develops, as I am sure many have experienced, a life of its own, a confidence, a free and friendly atmosphere where the therapists feel free to be themselves, and, as Balint (1957) wrote, the therapist is encouraged to have "the courage of his own stupidity". Enid Balint (1976) in her Freud Memorial Lecture at University College in London, said a similar thing, quoting a grateful GP who, after leaving one of the seminars, said in later years that the seminars had given him "a preparedness to be daft". I suppose what he and she meant by that was that he learned to value his own free-associative processes, his own primary processes, which is the idea, as I understand it, behind the flash technique, written up in "Six minutes for the patient" (Balint & Norell, 1973): the whole idea of the intuitive flash about a patient. Of course, this is about a patient who has been known for a long time by the GP; very different, I would wager, from Lacanian intuitive flashes, when the person is not so well known. In confirmation of this view, Enid Balint writes,

> I must emphasize that brief interviews of this kind have been studied in the setting of general practice only when an ongoing relationship between the doctor and his patient is customary so that although the flash itself is brief the relationship in which it occurs is long. [Balint & Norell, 1973, pp. 163–164]

In these kinds of seminar groups it is inherent that the leader of the group will hold back from making his own comments. This reduces the risk of dependence on the leader, with all the problems of idealization and consequent envy of the expert. The leader is, rather, a facilitator, making full use of the creativity of the group. He encourages the others to speak; he does not offer himself as the expert; he is the gardener; he is not the jug, pouring information in. "It is the aim of the psychoanalyst leader to keep the work going, i.e. to help the doctors share their observations, their ideas, to notice the existence of overlooked and obscure problems and contradictions" (Balint, 1976, p. 40). There is a phrase Balint (1957) often repeated: that such seminars and such training demand a "limited though considerable change of personality". Well, not all of us would hope for much more in psychotherapy, so there is obviously something very like psychotherapy taking place there.

Re-enactment in supervision

Several authors, including Balint (1957) and Searles (1955) talk of the idea about the patient–doctor relationship or client–therapist relationship being repeated by the therapist in relation to the supervisor in supervision. In thinking about this, my impression is that it does not happen so much in ongoing supervision of psychotherapy cases which have been formally assessed and selected as suitable for psychotherapy, put on a waiting-list, and then taken off the waiting-list by a therapist and supervisor. But it happens much more, and much more obviously, when the therapist has a free choice of case to present, such as in the Balint seminars, when Balint began "Who's got a case?"; or in the kind of seminars, which many of us have run, where trainees come to discuss any patient that they are having a problem with. The cases, having, therefore, been plucked out of the trainees' heads in response to some internal pressure, are much more likely to represent an aspect of the therapists themselves.

Recently, I had a very good opportunity of seeing this during a course for psychiatrists and psychotherapists who were hoping to learn more about supervision. One group was quite advanced and experienced: some psychoanalysts, some psychiatrists, some psychotherapists, who brought problems they had in supervising others. They were not bringing ongoing cases repeatedly, but because they chose them once-off, in response to some pressure, perhaps without being aware of it, they brought what the current problem was in the relationship between supervisor and supervisee. And it is quite remarkable to me how, in one weekend, three out of four supervisor–supervisee problems represented parallel patient–therapist problems all the way down the line.

(i) A female supervisor presented the problem of supervising a male therapist who had chosen to present a male patient with premature ejaculation. The problem the female supervisor was experiencing was that the therapist all the time insisted on being in control of the situation, making all his own decisions about therapy, including arranging to see the wife of his patient without even consulting the supervisor to see if that was appropriate. We felt in the seminar that the therapist was repeating his patient's problem of rushing to conclusions, that is, premature ejaculation, and not letting his female supervisor get any satisfaction from a proper exchange and relationship with him.

(ii) A female supervisor spoke about a male therapist who had a young female patient, who had been very suicidal throughout adolescence, while the patient's parents had been quarrelling and finally separating. It transpired that the male therapist also had a teenage daughter and he, the therapist, had recently divorced. And then the supervisor went on to say how difficult it all was for her because of her own recent divorce.

(iii) A male supervisor presented the problem he was having with a male therapist who had a female patient. The female patient was being seen only once every three weeks, and we all wondered why on earth he had chosen to discuss this supervision about a patient being seen every three weeks, rather than another female patient that the same therapist was seeing every week. Then it appeared that the therapist was about to drop this patient in one month, when the therapist was leaving the hospital. Further, it turned out that the therapist (supervisor and therapist were working in isolation) also provided mutual supervision from time to time for the supervisor. So, the patient was about to lose a therapist, and the supervisor was about to lose his supervisee and co-supervisor. Moreover, the whole institution was under threat of closure because of lack of funds. So we felt the supervisor was really bringing to the seminar his own loss in the guise of the patient's loss.

What I am saying is that where people freely choose a problem to talk about, the problem very much may represent an aspect of themselves and be repeated in the supervisory session.

Discussion

This paper arose out of an attempt to provide some parameters for discussion at a conference. As it evolved, it became something more like a tribute, especially to ideas associated with Winnicott and Michael Balint, and particularly to the latter's contributions to methods of teaching psychotherapy in group supervision seminars. Winnicott (1971) said, "Psychotherapy is not making clever and apt interpretations".

The same might be said of supervision of psychotherapy. It should not merely be an opportunity for the supervisor to be cleverer than the trainee, but it should facilitate the trainee's own thinking around the case. In supervision seminarsm the group process adds another creative dimension to this, as others contribute their own ideas and responses in free discussion.

The response of the therapist to the patient and the response of the supervisor and/or other seminar members to the presentation by the therapist, particularly as illustrated in the above section on re-enactment, have been considered here, using the concepts of transference, countertransference, and role re-enactment. In discussing such phenomena, others might consider using the concept of projective identification. However, as Ogden (1979) points out, though introduced by Melanie Klein in 1946, this concept is often avoided by others because of the great variety of meanings attached to the term. Full exploration and clarification of this issue are beyond the scope of this paper, which has been more concerned with styles and parameters of supervision that aim to facilitate the trainee therapist's own innate potential capacities.

Commentary (GW) on Chapter Seven: A brief history of psychotherapy in the British National Health Service: how can psychotherapists influence psychiatry?

his chapter provides an essential commentary that charts the emergence of psychotherapy in the NHS in the UK in the latter part of the twentieth century against the backdrop of key institutions, players, and places that informed the progress of public sector psychotherapy. Some of the "newer" developments that Pedder refers to here, such as the establishment of non-medical adult psychotherapists in the NHS, have since become embedded, and we can see how the psychotherapy profession has moved on a pace when we look at the cornerstones that Pedder situates here. The account offers a roll-call, or a family tree, of the key agents in psychoanalytic psychotherapy that highlights the medical hegemony that carried forward psychotherapy in the NHS. The chapter makes for necessary reading for anyone, medical or allied, interested in what has become of psychotherapy in the NHS. And, perhaps more importantly, from Pedder's account of ancestry here, there is a history to consider as a basis for what yet will become.

As well as working as a consultant psychotherapist at the Maudsley Hospital, one of the leading institutions in the training of mental health professionals, Pedder was an active member of the

Rugby Conference, the forerunner organization in the 1970s that set in place the accrediting process of psychotherapists, later to become the United Kingdom Council for Psychotherapy (UKCP). In the pre-UKCP Rugby Conference work, Pedder was an influential figure. He was also one of the founders of the Association of Psychoanalytic Psychotherapy (APP), set up originally in 1981 by a small group of London consultant psychiatrists who wanted to cement psychoanalytic psychotherapy into the training of psychiatrists, identifying the interested parties and their credentials, and then later the establishment of psychoanalytic psychotherapy more generally in the NHS. As a founding member of the APP in the NHS, Pedder's abiding interest has been to make accessible psychodynamic and psychoanalytic ideas to a multi-professional audience, in turn making dynamic psychotherapy available to a wider number of patients. From a handful of medical members, the APP now has wide membership of over 800 across a range of disciplines.

Pedder was also instrumental in the development of the UKCP, and throughout his career he remained committed to it when many of his psychoanalytic colleagues were steering a different course. At the APP AGM in 1998, he spoke up to recommend that the APP remain inclusive with regard to the UKCP, rather than singularly backing the British Confederation of Psychotherapy (BCP). The concern was to prevent any further fracturing of the attempts at unifying the psychotherapy profession. This view was not heeded at the time, and for a while only BCP members were able to be full members of the APP. However, it was only a matter of time before the APP opened up its full membership to UKCP members, and it is fair to say the APP has since become the inclusive umbrella organization that Pedder hoped for.

We can see, in this chapter, how Pedder stretched his interest in advancing psychotherapy practice beyond medical provision to envisage a range of multi-disciplinary stakeholders. He refers to Professor Bob Cawley (1977), his general psychiatrist colleague at the Maudsley, who argued that levels of psychotherapy should be apparent in the practice of all mental health professionals, ranging from talking therapy skills at an ordinary level of everyday intervention (Level 1), through to the skills of the career psychotherapist (Level 3) with specialist training. Pedder anticipates the academic progress here in relation to Masters degree level of preparation. It is notable that he considers crucial the role of what he refers to as senior institutions, such as the Tavistock Clinic, and senior professionals, such as psychiatrists, whom he sees as the gatekeepers of the psychotherapy profession. It does raise the question of leadership, if not the question of ownership of psychotherapy. Even if Pedder's view point might seem elitist, there can be no doubting his passionate commitment and track record in the NHS, and his own facilitative leadership in seeding a more accessible version of psychotherapy in the public sphere. In this chapter, he takes us back to the early decisions that some organizations took in electing to join the NHS or not, and certainly one wonders what might have been had the Institute of Psychoanalysis decided to join the NHS alongside the Cassel and the Tavistock.

It is sobering to read Pedder's account, in so far as we see that only a handful of organizations had a stake in NHS psychotherapy in the early days. By comparison, today there are a vast number of organizations delivering psychotherapy trainings with practitioners from a wider range of professional backgrounds. As he points out, it was only in the late 1970s that introductory textbooks, dedicated to the broad application of outpatient psychotherapy practice, were published. Compared to the longer lineage of psychotherapy in private practice, NHS psychotherapy is shown to be a recent event, if not quite a novel project. Today, there is a highly competitive climate for the psychotherapies and a new range of psychotherapies vying for position. The agenda for increasing access to psychological therapies (IAPT), and especially the positioning of cognitive–behaviour therapy, which is enjoying something of a boom, are worth contextualizing with the development that Pedder describes. Approaches that promise quicker, shorter, and cheaper treatments have been too easily contrasted with the practices of dynamic and exploratory psychotherapies, which have developed a reputation—albeit erroneously—for slower, longer-term practice. Twenty-five years after the establishment of the APP, psychoanalytic psychotherapy is more vulnerable than ever, especially where service commissioning is tallied to the recommendations in the National Institute for Clinical Excellence (NICE) guidelines, which, for the present, favour CBT. Dr Ronnie Doctor, Chair of the APP 2006–2010, is clear about the threats to psychoanalytic psychotherapy and what needs to be done:

APP Council has become aware of the threat posed to psychoanalytic work in the NHS, represented by the current NICE Guidelines. This is not a phenomenon that is isolated in the NHS, it is to do with how evidence based medicine is driving change in healthcare systems across all developed countries. For our part though, we have to face up to how we have become defensive, unconsciously perhaps, about making the case for our work in ways that can be heard. Thus the APP has been put into the position of having to develop a strategic plan to counter this threat. The first step in becoming involved in reviewing the current NICE Guidelines and to participate in new ones, was to register as a NICE Guidelines Stakeholder. We also became aware that there were gaps in the APP with regard to its Research and Development section and it was decided that one of the primary aims of the APP was to prioritise research and development (R&D), with the specific purpose of developing random control trials and to coordinate an active community of research practitioners and make partnership links e.g. with the Tavistock & Portman NHS Trust. It was also decided to set up the APP as an NHS lobbying group, as it was found that the existing NICE Guidelines had been drawn up using criteria that favoured research into CBT and against clinical outcomes for psychodynamic treatment. We need to put the argument that changes in these criteria are necessary to redress the bias. Finally, if the APP is to act as an association that can influence NHS commissioners, which we need to do to protect our members' jobs, we have to develop expertise working at the political interface as well as the clinical interface. The APP's remit allows it to be instrumental in bringing together professional organisations, who can begin to translate a step-care approach so that patients are offered a choice of effective therapy options. Psychoanalytic organisations need the support and goodwill of the rest of the field, and to work at building alliances and common agendas. [personal communication, Doctor, 2008]

Organizationally speaking, and strategically for the profession of dynamic psychotherapies in the NHS, perhaps there does need to be more punch from those who represent the profession in the healthcare market. Pedder does indeed refer to "punch" in this chapter when he talks about Wally Joffe's unique clinical capacity to "hold patients up with one hand and punch them hard with the other". It is a rather powerful and somewhat controversial description of therapeutic demeanour, but it might be apposite here when it comes to reflecting on the market predicament of psychoanalytic psychotherapy. We see later in the chapter that Pedder tries to reconcile notions of psychotherapeutic disposition, which he frames as a dialectic of (i) "tough-mindedness", the scientific approach, and (ii) "tender-mindedness". The tender-minded approach to the market probably does not work as well as the tough-minded approach.

It is worth reflecting on Pedder's account of the history of psychotherapy in light of the challenge today, because he pays heed to the question of whether the NHS psychotherapist should stand as a distinct professional identity. He discusses how psychiatrists oscillated as to whether they should be consultant psychotherapists, and he refers to the debates in the British Psychological Society about psychologists already thinking of themselves as psychotherapists. In Pedder's account, there is little of the bunker mentality that exists of late in relation to the territorial warfare in the NHS when it comes to psychological therapies, where, in some cases, counsellors, psychologists, and psychotherapists have had to retrain in cognitive–behavioural therapy or risk losing their jobs. Pedder does not seem to convey any of the entrenchment we hear sometimes in the new denominations about whether an approach is properly pure, integrative, or person centred, or whatever. There are alternatives, Pedder reminds us, that core professionals might choose to practise in whatever they feel comfortable. There is a sense that the debate about "who is called what" may actually be a distraction from the mission of ensuring that all professionals think in depth about their work, where psychoanalytic ideas can be brought to bear without the formalization of identities.

The final question as to how psychotherapy shapes psychiatry takes the influence of the three Bs, as he calls them: Bion, Balint, and Bowlby, as a starting point. Given that these three male figures form the backdrop for his formulation of the shape of the profession, there is an absorbing and intriguing discussion about the masculine and the feminine in the psychotherapy profession. Pedder vitalizes the values of poetry and romanticism, counterpoising rational sciences, and though one thinks that his gender-specific view might be controversial, I actually find it far from controversial. Rather, Pedder's positioning of gender differentials in the approach of psychotherapists offers an enlightening discussion about difference that might throw some light on the difficulties that psychoanalytic psychotherapy experiences in the welfare sphere. That is to say, the tender-mindedness of the profession, certainly in the NHS, means psychotherapy is seen as a soft target for services cuts, the closure of the Henderson Hospital being a recent example. Pedder's idea that leadership might be left in the hands of the medical doctor offers more controversy, but does draw attention to a debate about the progress of the medical model, and where psychotherapy is best situated: allied to medicine or otherwise? Pedder favours medical hegemony, and many might agree that this is perhaps the safest place to situate the future direction of psychotherapy. Pedder leaves us with the teasing question that reads like a good transprofessional exam question for any student of dynamic counselling and psychotherapy: "Would Freud have been so influential if he had not been a doctor?"

A brief history of psychotherapy in the British National Health Service: how can psychotherapists influence psychiatry?

T his outline sketch of the history of psychotherapy in the NHS was an introduction to a half-day session on "Psychotherapy in the Health Service". It is argued that the history of psychotherapy in the NHS cannot be seen in perspective, both before the inception of the NHS as well as since, and without considering psychotherapy outside the NHS as well as within, since the links between the two are vital in many areas. The demand for psychotherapy outside the NHS is probably strong partly because of the poor provision within.

It is necessary to consider different levels of psychotherapy (Cawley, 1977); the many varieties of psychotherapy, individual and group, brief and long-term, family and marital, behavioural and cognitive, and also the many disciplines involved in the delivery of psychotherapy at various levels. In terms of general definitions, I often think of Alexander's (1957) statement, "Everyone who tries to encourage a despondent friend or to reassure a panicky child practises psychotherapy". And then there are special definitions, such as that of Sutherland (1968):

> By psychotherapy I refer to a personal relationship with a professional person in which those in distress can share and explore the

underlying nature of their troubles, and possibly change some of the determinants of these, through experiencing unrecognized forces in themselves.

Although psychotherapy initially developed as a separate (medical) speciality within psychiatry, now there are many other disciplines involved. The contributions of the different disciplines is considered briefly herein—doctors, whether psychiatrists or general practitioners, psychologists, social workers, and child psychotherapists. Finally, it is noted that, *de facto*, a new discipline of adult (non-medical) psychotherapy has emerged within the NHS. I shall argue that the main thrust of psychotherapy in the UK has been dynamic psychotherapy, with its historical origins in psychoanalysis and its applications. Prominent in any history would be the two institutions, the Institute of Psychoanalysis and the Tavistock Clinic. Their influence may be regarded by some as wholly beneficial or largely beneficial, as I would think, but others might think of them as largely or wholly unhelpful. Their legacy is situated here.

Historical trajectory

We need to think of different levels of psychotherapy, from the more supportive to the more exploratory. In discussing psychotherapy, I have often found it helpful to use Cawley's (1977) idea of three different levels (Levels 1–3) of psychotherapy and then a fourth category of behavioural psychotherapy. Level 1 would be what all good health professionals do, which might otherwise be known as counselling or supportive psychotherapy; Level 2 would be what the best members of the core professions do, whether they are psychiatrists, psychologists, social workers, or nurses; and Level 3, a more specialist level of career psychotherapy, otherwise referred to as dynamic psychotherapy. These three might be seen as deepening levels of psychotherapy. Cawley also included a Level 4, behaviour therapy, as a separate category, but 3 and 4 also come together now, in fields such as family and marital therapy and psycho-sexual counselling. Some people object to this idea of levels, arguing paradoxically that supportive psychotherapy (Level 1) is quite the most difficult to deliver, and needs the most training. But I think it is useful to think of these different levels of depth which might also parallel different levels, or stages, of training, from the first undergraduate degree to, second, a core professional training, and then some specialist post-graduate training. It relates to the difference between psychotherapy training and practice expected for all members of the helping professions, and specialized training for psychotherapists who wish to be specially recognized as such. This reflects the difference between Levels 2 and 3 of Cawley's levels of psychotherapy practice. In psychiatry, it is the difference between general professional training at the registrar level and specialist training for senior registrars (future consultants) at the higher training level.

General professional training is the concern of the Royal College of Psychiatrists, which has revised its guidelines for the training of general psychiatrists in psychotherapy, first appearing in 1971 and revised in 1986 and 1993 (Royal College of Psychiatrists, 1993). Higher training for senior registrars has been the business of the Joint Committee on Higher Psychiatric Training. If we proceed to the registration of psychotherapists, this difference (between general and specialist training) would also be reflected in Sieghart's (1978) proposals for indicative rather than functional registration. Few people want functional registration, which would limit who can do psychotherapy, but indicative registration makes more sense, where nobody could call themselves a specialist psycho-therapist who had not undergone specialist training—a specific post-graduate training following an initial period of basic profes-sional training.

Though my brief here is the history of psychotherapy in the NHS, this history cannot be seen in perspective without consider-ing psychotherapy both before the inception of the NHS as well as since, and without considering psychotherapy outside the NHS as well as within it, since the links between the two are vital in many areas. This interrelationship is especially strong in matters of train-ing. I am thinking of the Institute of Psycho-Analysis in London, established thirty years before the NHS, and the Institutes of Group Analysis and Family Therapy, founded more recently. The Scottish Institute of Human Relations (SIHR) was founded in the early 1970s by Jock Sutherland when he retired early from the Tavistock and went back to Edinburgh. The SIHR has been an independent organization providing training in analytic psychotherapy on a multi-disciplinary basis, relied upon by senior registrars in psychotherapy over a wide area in Scotland, from Glasgow, Edinburgh, and Dundee, and from Newcastle in the North of England. Then, apart from independent analytic trainings, also outside or alongside the NHS, are the university-based diplomas and MSc courses in psychotherapy, a more recent phenomenon from the 1980s (Pedder, 1989). I am thinking of the MSc at St Georges, Leeds, and Warwick, and certificate or diploma psychotherapy courses at Newcastle, Oxford, Guy's, and South Trent. A further example of the links between within and without the NHS is in the field of child psychotherapy training. In London, child psychotherapy training began in 1949, both within the NHS, at the Tavistock Clinic, and without at Anna Freud's Hampstead Clinic.

Next, a note about the emergence of psychotherapy as a separate speciality within psychiatry. In the mid-nineteenth century, psychiatry was largely an affair of mental hospitals. Patients were removed from sight, beyond city boundaries. Before the First World War, a few exceptional individuals became interested in psychotherapy and psychoanalysis, and some, such as Ernest Jones, travelled to Vienna to study with Freud. In the First World War, there was an increased interest in neurotic, non-psychotic disorders, otherwise known as functional disorders, or shell shock. It was under this impetus that, soon after the war, the Tavistock Clinic and Cassel Hospital were founded. Then, in the Second World War, there was a further acceleration of interest in psychodynamic and psychoanalytic ideas. Bion, Foulkes, and Main's contributions are well known, and it was their work in Army psychiatry and in the Northfields Experiment which led to the development of therapeutic community ideas.

When the National Health Service was inaugurated in 1948, the Cassel Hospital, the Portman and Tavistock Clinics, all elected to join the NHS. The London Clinic of Psychoanalysis, linked to the Institute of Psychoanalysis, chose to remain separate. Psychiatrists in teaching hospitals were still known as physicians in psychological medicine, and psychiatry was still often seen as a branch of medicine and neurology. It was not until 1971 that the Royal College of Psychiatrists was founded, evolving from the older

RMPA (Royal Medico-Psychological Association). The former Psychotherapy and Social Psychiatry Section of the RMPA became the Psychotherapy Section of the new College. In 1975, psychotherapy was recognized by the then Department of Health and Social Security as a separate speciality, and took its place alongside the other specialities of general psychiatry, child and adolescent psychiatry, forensic psychiatry, and mental handicap. Each speciality has felt this differentiation to be important, in order that each might have more control of its separate manpower allocations and of its separate senior registrar, higher training posts. Old-age psychiatry went through a comparable evolution.

Before 1975, many consultants at the Tavistock, Cassel, and elsewhere still held contracts as consultant psychiatrists. There was a campaign in the Royal College of Psychiatrists Psychotherapy section to get them to change these to "consultant psychotherapist". This was important, because the number of senior registrars in psychotherapy, as in any speciality, is geared to the number of consultants. In other words, without more consultant psychotherapists, there could not be more senior registrars. That point is often forgotten. For example, Wilkinson (1984), objecting to the growth of psychotherapy and the apparent rise in the number of psychotherapists in the mid-1970s, failed to note that this was mostly because psychiatrists were being re-designated as psychotherapists. The actual expansion of persons in the field was a small steady one, well below recommended norms from the Royal College of Psychiatrists. In the 1970s, the Joint Committee on Higher Psychiatric Training (JCHPT) came into being, with its separate speciality advisory committees to oversee higher training programmes at the senior registrar level in each of the psychiatric specialities, including psychotherapy. In 1987, the Joint Planning Advisory Committee (JPAC) reviewed the numbers of senior registrar posts in psychotherapy. At that time, there were sixteen full-time posts plus eight part-time married women's posts. A further thirteen extra posts were allocated, and a further four part-time posts. These were intended to be evenly distributed around the country. Oxford and Guy's were among the first into the field. Although it was perfectly fair that such posts should be evenly distributed around the country, in practice, this has remained problematic in terms of access and training beyond major centres.

It has been questioned as to whether we need a separate speciality of psychotherapy at all. Some say psychotherapy should have
remained part of general psychiatry. Indeed, there are psychoanalysts and psychotherapists who have functioned as general psychiatrists, running an ordinary psychiatric admission ward. This view
was formerly taken, particularly in the southwest of England, that
a separate speciality of psychotherapy was not needed, because
psychotherapy should be part of general psychiatry. That may be a
fine millennial view, but until we get there, I think specialist
psychotherapists are needed as flag carriers for the speciality.

I have been speaking of the development of psychotherapy as a
separate medical speciality within psychiatry. Clearly, medical
psychotherapists are neither the only doctors, nor are doctors the
only discipline, involved in providing psychotherapy. Among
doctors, possibly the greatest amount of psychotherapy at Levels 1
and 2 is carried out by general practitioners, a third of whose
patients have primary emotional disorders, though only one in
twenty of these are referred on to specialist services. Gask and
McGrath (1989) reviewed the relationship between psychotherapy
and general practice, and the development of liaison psychotherapy
in general practice. They said that, in part, the pressure for the
development of liaison psychotherapy stemmed from the increasing recognition that psychotherapy in the NHS had a much wider
definition and range of application than psychoanalysis or the
services offered by the specialist psychotherapy units. However,
they do go on to acknowledge in their review the pioneer work of
Michael Balint in this field. Another review by Sibbald, Addington-
Hall, Brenneman, and Freeling (1993) revealed that around thirty
per cent of GP practices had employed some kind of primary care
counsellor or psychotherapist, more especially in large and training
practices functioning from health centres. These practitioners were
drawn from community psychiatric nurses and clinical psychologists, as well as counsellors who were not "core professionals".

Turning to other non-medical disciplines, psychologists and
social workers in particular contribute at all three levels. The Royal
College of Psychiatry's Psychotherapy Section's *Future of Psychotherapy Services* document (1991) detailed the idea of a core team of
three whole-time-equivalent psychotherapists per district, of which
one might be medical. This was a relatively modest proposal

compared with other estimations (e.g., Richardson, 1989), which argued the case for seven psychiatrists, also seven clinical psychologists, and seven psychotherapists for an average district of 200,000. The British Psychological Society (BPS) was initially unenthusiastic about the issue of registration of psychotherapists, arguing that all psychologists were already psychotherapists, so that it was unnecessary. True, they may all be Level 2 psychotherapists, but not all are specialist trained in either dynamic or behavioural psychotherapy, any more than psychiatrists are. However, their particular position and contribution was recognized initially by the United Kingdom Standing Conference for Psychotherapy (UKSCP), the forerunner to the United Kingdom Council for Psychotherapy (UKCP), which made the BPS and British Association of Social Workers (BASW), along with the Royal College of Psychiatrists, special members of UKSCP, which emerged through the annual "Rugby" psychotherapy conferences held throughout the 1980s (Pedder, 1989).

It is striking that the professions of these special members paralleled the entry requirement, certainly up until the late 1980s, of many independent psychotherapy trainings and Master's level academic programmes. And in diploma level psychotherapy courses, applicants were mostly from the core professions of psychiatry, psychology, and social work. Psychologists were particularly notable for their contribution to behavioural and cognitive therapy in the 1970s, though many became more interested in dynamic psychotherapy later. Social workers, especially in their casework in the 1950s, were strongly influenced by psychodynamic ideas, with an emphasis on the importance of the setting, of reliability, and of good supervision. Some of this was lost following the Seebohm reorganization of social workers in the 1970s and the introduction of generic social work. But the Group for the Advancement of Psychodynamics and Psychotherapy in Social Work (GAPPS) was founded in 1971 as a rallying point to rediscover this psychodynamic emphasis. Clearly, social workers have been under intense pressures, squeezed between child abuse cases and local authority financial cuts. So, it seems unlikely that social work will reinvent psychiatric social workers, let alone specialist psychotherapists.

Another historical note on publications and academic developments is worth reviewing: in a hundred years, historians would get

some idea of the time sequence in which the main types of psychotherapy emerged in the UK from the dates when the principal journals dealing with them were founded. The *British Journal of
Psychiatry* first appeared in 1850, as the *Journal of Mental Science*. The
International Journal of Psycho-Analysis was founded in 1919 and the
British Journal of Medical Psychology, the journal of the Medical
Section of the BPS, which was a meeting-place for psychotherapists
between the wars, was founded in 1927. *Human Relations*, the journal of the Tavistock Institute of Human Relations, was founded in
1947; the *Journal of Child Psychotherapy* in 1963; *Group Analysis*, the
journal of the Institute of Group Analysis, started in 1969;
Behavioural Psychotherapy, the journal of the British Association of
Behavioural Psychotherapy, started in 1973; the *Journal of Family
Therapy*, journal of the Association of Family Therapists (AFT),
started in 1979. There were no separate textbooks of psychotherapy
from the UK until the late 1970s. Then, in 1979, four appeared
together: Bloch's (1979) *An Introduction to the Psychotherapies*; Brown
and Pedder's *Introduction to Psychotherapy* (1979); Malan's *Psychotherapy and the Science of Psychodynamics* (1979); and Storr's *The Art
of Psychotherapy* (1979) all came out in the same year. In the 1980s,
four journals appeared roughly together: *Psychoanalytic Psychotherapy* (the journal of the Association for Psychoanalytic Psychotherapy, which was founded in 1981); *The British Journal of
Psychotherapy*; *The International Journal of Therapeutic Communities*;
and, more without the NHS, *Free Associations*.

So, there were notable developments in publishing, but less in
formal academic developments and research, with only a few
senior lecturer posts in psychotherapy in the UK and, of two chairs
advertised, only one was filled. When the detailed history of
psychotherapy comes to be written, as I have already indicated, I
think two institutions will remain central, whatever ambivalence
and mixed feelings surround them. These are the Institute of Psychoanalysis, with its Society and Clinic, which remain outside the
NHS, and the Tavistock, which joined the National Health Service
but remains, as from its start, somewhere between psychoanalysis,
medicine, and psychiatry. The view that all forms of dynamic
psychotherapy historically stem from psychoanalysis may need
qualification, as Ellenberger (1970) suggests, but Freud focused
trends in thought about psychic conflict that were around in the late

nineteenth century, and addressed these in a fresh way to the problems he encountered as a neurologist dealing with hysteria. Since then, psychoanalytic ideas have been applied in individual, group, family, and marital therapy, brief therapy, and child psychotherapy. The Tavistock has been central in all these developments and applications in the UK.

The Tavistock was founded in the 1920s, as a result of the vision of Hugh Crichton-Miller, who became the first director (Dicks, 1970). It was in response to the problems of dealing with shell-shock cases after the First World War. It was set up to be somewhere between psychoanalysis and orthodox psychiatry, which is where I think it has remained. It had early links with the Cassel Hospital for Functional Nervous Disorders, as it was called, which had a similar history—founded after the First World War. There were similar links with the West End Hospital for Nervous Diseases, the forerunner of the Paddington Clinic (which later renamed itself the Parkside Clinic). By the 1930s, the Tavistock was training members of the new professions of clinical psychology and psychiatric social work. In the 1930s, too, members founded the Davidson Clinic in Edinburgh and the Institute for the Scientific Treatment of Delinquency (ISTD), which later became the Portman Clinic. In 1934, J. R. Rees took over as the second director, and the standing of the Tavistock in the late 1930s was such that he became Psychiatric Adviser to the Army in the war.

The work of Wilfred Bion, Tom Main, and Michael Foulkes in the Northfields' Experiment during the war is an important cornerstone in the history of NHS psychotherapy. Foulkes went on after the war to become Consultant Psychotherapist at the Maudsley, and to found the Institute of Group Analysis. Main became Medical Director of the Cassel Hospital, a therapeutic community in South West London. Bion, who was perhaps particularly respected due to his First World War experience as a tank commander, and known for his introduction of group methods in officer selection during the war, later became Chairman of the Interim Medical Committee at the Tavistock after the war, where he introduced group methods, influencing Maxwell Jones and others, who took the ideas to the Henderson and other therapeutic communities.

In 1947, Jock Sutherland became Medical Director of the Tavistock and Chair of the Adult Department. Bowlby became Deputy

Director and Chair of the Children's Department. Bowlby's influence has been enormous in many fields: his work on maternal separation, attachment, and loss, his backing of the Robertsons and their work in child care and children going to hospital, has profoundly influenced practice. Bowlby was also influential in the founding of child psychotherapy. The third B, Michael Balint, was responsible for the founding of the Family Discussion Bureau, which has subsequently gone on to become the Institute of Marital Studies, where he and Enid Balint did their early work together. His work with general practitioner seminars in the 1950s is well known. That style of working continued when he retired from the Tavistock and went to work at University College Hospital, where he developed medical student psychotherapy and supervision, along with Heinz Wolf (Pedder, 1986). Balint's third influence—his workshop on brief, focal psychotherapy—led to Malan's studies in brief psychotherapy.

In 1967, the new Tavistock was built in an era when Kenneth Robinson was the Labour Government's Minister of Health. The Child Guidance Training Centre was included under its roof. The Portman Clinic was not, though it was located close by. In 1968, when Sutherland went to Edinburgh and founded the Scottish Institute of Human Relations, it became affectionately referred to as the "MacTavi".

Child psychotherapy's history, very interestingly, parallels the development of the new profession of adult non-medical psychotherapist. It begins in the UK before the war, with Melanie Klein's arrival and her work in the mid-1920s, and then Anna Freud's arrival in the late 1930s. Discussions on training were delayed until after the war. Some medical doctors did not approve of the idea of lay psychotherapists at all, and some psychologists did not see the need of a new profession. However, it was supported by Bowlby, and in 1949 the first two trainings started: inside the NHS, at the Tavistock, supported by Bowlby, outside the NHS at Anna Freud's Hampstead Clinic. At first, it was called the Provisional Association of Child Psychotherapists (Non-Medical), the "non-medical" put there at the insistence of the medical profession. The provisional association had a medical advisory council and the training council had to have equal numbers of medical and non-medical members. In 1951, they dropped "provisional" from the title. In 1972, they dropped "non-medical" from the title, and in 1977, they dropped their medical advisory council. I mention child psychotherapy because it closely parallels the development of a profession of adult non-medical psychotherapists. The parallels hardly need spelling out. It has become clear that, *de facto*, a new discipline of adult (non-medical) psychotherapist has emerged within the NHS. In the late 1980s, there were only about twenty such posts, both in London—Willesden and Portman Clinic—and outside London in Nottingham, Portsmouth, and Lincoln. Radicals in such positions wanted instant parity in all respects with medical psychotherapists, and wanted to drop the "non-medical" tag. Others, perhaps reactionaries, resisted the development, in the same way that the debate was held in the child psychotherapy profession.

This brief outline sketch of the history of psychotherapy in the NHS has argued that the history of psychotherapy in the NHS cannot be seen in perspective without considering psychotherapy both before the inception of the NHS and since. It is also necessary to consider the way in which various organizational developments and sub-systems of psychotherapy have been influential. We need to consider psychotherapy outside the NHS as well as within, as the links between the two have been vital in many areas of training and theoretical development. The demand for psychotherapy outside the NHS has probably been strong partly because of the poor provision within.

How can psychotherapists influence psychiatry

So, how can psychotherapists influence psychiatry? Many of us are engaged as psychoanalysts and psychotherapists in this task of trying to influence psychiatry in various ways in various Health Service settings. One could imagine different cultures in different countries—and maybe in different parts of Europe—where the question could not be asked. Psychotherapy is an inherent part of psychiatry, but it is still all too rare across the UK. Even if, in the future, psychotherapy were to become an altogether separate profession, the question would still remain: how can psychotherapists influence psychiatry? We begin by looking at the tension between psychiatry and psychodynamics, a tension that, as in a marriage, may be more or less creative or destructive.

We are all familiar with the very different positions in psychiatry that easily become polarized, often called the organic *vs.* the psychodynamic view. On the one hand, we have the somatic, medical view; on the other hand, the more psychological view. On the one hand, the objective, scientific point of view; on the other, the more subjective, empathic, hermeneutic point of view. Rodman (1986) argued that "The therapist stands between the objectivity of science and the inwardness of poetry". These two views you could see as the more "tough-minded" scientific approach and the more "tender-minded" approach. We might see these as the more masculine *vs.* the more feminine point of view. Many people regard that analysis as highly sexist, and they prefer to speak of the approach of the dominant *vs.* the non-dominant cerebral hemisphere, or to talk of the difference between convergent and divergent forms of thinking. I think it is actually, in longer, historical perspective, part of an old unresolved tension between the rational and romantic view of man, which we still see traces of in this tension between organic and psychoanalytic orientations within psychiatry.

The earlier emphasis on rational thinking, following Descartes, led to the Enlightenment of the eighteenth century, but it devalued imaginative and emotional life, so that a natural reaction was the Romantic movement of the early nineteenth century (Pedder, 1989). Symington (1986), in a chapter on "Freud the Romantic", suggested that Freud's genius was due to his capacity to integrate two traditions, the Romantic and the scientific, which had previously been in antagonism to each other. Science and Romanticism come together in psychoanalysis, but psychoanalysis to this day remains a scandal to the natural scientist, as it also is to the Romantic (p. 83). Ideally, psychiatry might combine both rational and romantic points of view, or both masculine and feminine perspectives. But Denis Hill, late Professor of Psychiatry at the Maudsley, was somewhat dispirited about the possibility:

> There has always seemed to be, unfortunately, an antithesis between the strengths of an academic in psychiatry and the strengths he has for therapeutic skills, psychotherapeutic skills in particular. But there is an antithesis. The two ways of thinking do not appear to be compatible. And I would be the last person to defend my academic brethren on the grounds that they are good

psychotherapists. I know they are not. In fact many of them are, for practical purposes, not therapists at all and don't wish to be. They don't wish to involve themselves very much with patients, which is a very sad thing, but there it is. When I was at the Maudsley I did my best to try to marry the different sides of psychiatry without the usual onset of contempt or mutual hostility. It is surprising, really, how mutual hostility persists in this country, despite every effort one makes to stop it. [Hill, 1982, p. 85]

Note he uses the word "marry" there, to relate these two opposite sides of psychiatry, and, indeed, he was married to a psychoanalyst. Now, we might argue that all psychiatrists should be both academics and psychotherapists in an ideal world. However, until we get there, psychotherapists are needed as a separate speciality as standard bearers. In a separate profession of psychotherapy, with its own pre-clinical colleges, as advocated by Freud (1926e) in "The question of lay analysis", students would study many subjects other than the biological sciences including, "the history of civilisation, mythology, the psychology of religion and the science of literature" (p. 246).

It is the vulnerability of patients and their pain and suffering that all of us in the helping professions were moved to try to alleviate, yet are always tempted to escape from, in various ways. Traditionally, in hospital, much of this pain and distress has been left to the nurse–mothers to cope with. Doctors escape in all kinds of ways: by prescribing investigations and drugs, by operating on unconscious patients, by research, administration, committees, or coming to conferences. I do not think any of us are guilt-free about this, in the different ways in which we are tempted to take flight from patients. This intolerable mental suffering of patients fuelled the crusade of people like William Sargant, to find the physical causes and treatments of psychiatric disorders. It was perhaps fired in him when, after a severe mental and physical collapse, he took up a job as a locum at Hanwell Mental Hospital, where he was appalled at the plight of patients and the impotence of the staff to alleviate their suffering (*British Medical Journal*, 1988). Stephen's (1988) recent book concerned a young woman who disappeared and the understandable distress and difficulty her family had in accepting the disappearance. The mother happened to know socially a psychiatrist trainee in Sargant's school, and asked his advice on how she and her husband should cope. "Keep busy," came his reply, "keep so busy you sleep from tiredness—you must not dwell on the pain and futility of it all." Psychotherapists take a different view. Psychotherapy stands for attempts to bear this pain and futility, and to support others in doing so, whether through supervision, through staff groups, or by encouraging the personal psychotherapy of the staff themselves.

I do not want to be misunderstood as saying that psychotherapy is just about empathy. This is one of the misunderstandings to which I think Winnicott was sometimes liable. Even within psychotherapy, male and female principles operate. Wolff (1971), following Winnicott, has written about the difference between doing to and being with patients—between a more paternal and a more maternal mode. Guntrip (1961), in discussing Winnicott's views on technique, said, "The position that seems to be emerging is that at all stages psychotherapy has to be an appropriate mixture of mothering (management) and analysis (giving insight)" (p. 413). Or, as I would see it, it is a mixture of feminine and masculine elements, both of which the analytic psychotherapist has to combine in him or herself. I had the fortunate experience of working, twenty years ago, as co-therapist in a psychotherapy group with W. G. Joffe, a few years before his death, which gave me the chance to observe his unique capacity to hold patients up with one hand and punch them hard with the other, combining his warm friendly humanity with shrewd analytic insights, a subtle blend of feminine and masculine traits which I think is an essence of psychotherapy. Steiner (1985) suggested the idea of the complementarity of the masculine theory, with the more feminine components of the holding situation of personal therapy, which both have a part to play: the holding therapy and the masculine theory. Bion has written about the analyst as both "probe", a rather masculine penetrative image, and "container", a more feminine function.

Much of the difficulties of psychotherapy in relation to psychiatry could be seen as similar to the differences that women and men have had in society. The way psychotherapy sometimes gets rather devalued and denigrated could be seen as similar to the way child-rearing has been regarded. Until the turn of the century, psychiatry was an affair of mental hospitals. At best, this was good custodial care, like the York Retreat in England. At worst, it led to all kinds of abuses and institutionalization. When Freud returned from Paris to Vienna in 1886, he set up in private practice as a neurologist and what followed is now our history. He rescued the neurotic patient from the public theatre of Charcot's demonstrations, and created the private space of the analytic consulting room, where hitherto unacknowledged aspects of man's inner world could be faced. We could say that Breuer and Freud, with the help of their remarkable patients, legitimized the expression and discharge of feelings in patients, and through the development of the concept of transference Freud provided a way of conceptualizing the awkward feelings which had troubled Breuer. The concept of countertransference legitimized the acknowledgement of feelings in the therapist. The latter was first thought of as an obstacle, as the therapist's unanalysed transference to the patient; and Freud took this no further. It was another generation or more before Heimann (1950) and others began turning attention to this second aspect of countertransference, which, far from being an obstacle, became an important tool in psychotherapy. Winnicott (1947) even legitimized the acknowledgement of hate in the countertransference.

As Michael and Enid Balint (1961) put it, what the doctor feels is part of his patient's illness. In other words, what the therapist feels is part of the patient's communication, conscious or unconscious. Obviously, this concept can all too easily be abused, so, to deal with the countertransference and sort out the primary and secondary varieties, personal analysis was thought desirable for psychotherapists. When the Balints started training social workers at the Tavistock Clinic, who on the whole had not had their own personal therapy, a way had to be found of dealing with the trainees' own personal feelings, without slipping too much into therapy. They adapted the Hungarian psychoanalytic training system, where the therapist and analyst were the same person: you talked about yourself on four days of the week and your patient on the fifth day of the week, so the patient was approached via the countertransference. The Balints did not allow notes in their seminars. They encouraged free-floating discussion, which relied on the therapists' feelings about their clients. The space for this free associative discussion needs to be a safe, protected space; just as the mother's primary maternal preoccupation with her infant needs the protection of the father, so does the therapist's primary therapeutic preoccupation with his patient need protection from outside intrusion.

So, I return from considering "being with" patients to consider what we need "to do for" them to protect this space—from maternal to more paternal functions. You may wish to argue whether we should seek this space in psychiatric treatments at all, and prefer, as some do, the development of psychoanalytical therapy entirely separately from psychiatry. This issue was much taken up by the "Rugby" Conference in psychotherapy, the annual conference that led to the inauguration of a Standing Conference for Psychotherapy in January 1989 (Pedder, 1990) where some non-medical psychotherapists immediately objected to the expression "non-medical", arguing that they were being defined by an absence or lack. We might return to the structuralist male–female argument, like a woman rightly objecting to being seen as a man without a penis.

So what further professional and organizational differentiations will occur in the future? If you remember that in the first two decades of the century, psychoanalysis stood relatively alone: child analysis developed in the 1920s and 1930s, group analysis in the 1940s, family and marital therapy, and brief forms of psychotherapy were post-war developments, there are bound to be further generational differentiations. But, if we want psychotherapy to remain in psychiatry, there are a number of more paternal political tasks to do with minding and mending fences that we need to attend to. This leads us back to the political and administrative sphere. If we are to ensure psychotherapy remains as part of psychiatry, and claims equal weight to other specialities, there are a lot of tasks to be undertaken and a need for medical hegemony. That is not to discount the contribution of other professions or the potential of the new profession of non-medical adult psychotherapists. But would Freud have been so influential if he had not been a doctor?

Commentary (GW) on Chapter Eight: Lines of advance: increasing access to psychoanalytic therapy

I n this chapter, we glean some of the philosophical underpin-
nings of Pedder's motivation to see an increased access to
psychological therapies and the background to his book, *Introduction to Psychotherapy*, co-authored with the late Dennis Brown.
Introduction to Psychotherapy has now been a staple text for psychotherapists across several generations since it was first published in
1979. The book was initially aimed at a widened gateway of
psychoanalytically informed practitioners, and became an introductory text for trainings in the fields of counselling, group, and
arts therapies, as well as formal psychoanalytic and psychotherapy
training. The title of this next chapter; "Lines of advance", is taken
from Pedder's Association of Psychoanalytic Psychotherapy (APP)
lecture in 1988, which was the second annual APP lecture and deep-
ens his debate about access to psychoanalytic therapy in the public
sphere. Pedder begins with his own interest in seeing psychoanalysis spread beyond the confines of London and, drawing on a
European history, Pedder asserts the place for a vitalized interest in
European psychotherapy. Freud's (1919a) paper; "Lines of advance
in psychoanalytic therapy", is the appealing backdrop for Pedder's
theoretical elaboration.

The chapter unfolds the ideal of psychotherapy for the masses. There is a brief history of the early days of the psychoanalytic movement and the struggle for acceptance. Pedder focuses on the International Psychoanalytic Association (IPA) Congress held in Budapest in the Hotel Gellert in 1918, and examines from there the Hungarian influence of Ferenczi, Klein, and Balint. It was at the Fifth IPA Congress that Freud first presented his paper "Lines of advance". The Budapest hotel was later to hold a particular significance for Pedder, because, in 1969, he gave his first paper to an international conference there. He admits that, at the time at least, he was more impressed by the wave machine in the outdoor swimming-pool than the history of the hotel!

Pedder considers Freud's idea of uniting the pure gold analysis with the copper alloy of more active therapeutic approaches. He pays heed to the philanthropy of Anton Von Freund in sponsoring psychoanalysis in Hungary. Pedder quotes from Freud at length, and the important passage where Freud develops a rather radical idea about the politics of privilege and his dream that one day psychoanalysis, in the service of mass welfare, might be free at point of delivery. This aspiration has been realized, at least to some extent, in public services across Europe, but most especially in the UK, where psychoanalytical ideas have been embedded in the NHS. Pedder sees psychoanalysts as the "lighthouse keepers" of psychoanalytic theory and practice, throwing beacons of light across dangerous waters. It is a memorable assertion, and summons up both the image of guidance, and also the remoteness of the psychoanalyst. Pedder acknowledges this: "psychoanalysts are good at keeping their torch alight but have not always been so good at offering its warmth to outsiders". He thinks that it is not enough to have remote psychoanalytic theory, and that there needs to be a wider work force of practitioners, or psychoanalytic sailors, as he puts it. He returns to the project of the Association of Psychoanalytic Psychotherapy (APP), which he sees as offering an alloy frame for disseminating and advancing psychoanalytic practice. With recourse to Shakespeare, and then Freud's references to the three caskets in *The Merchant of Venice*, Pedder points out that all that glistens is not gold. He charts the waves of change in psychotherapy, and particularly the emergence of non-medical psychotherapy, using the child psychotherapy profession as a particular case in point for the effect of radicalization.

It is worth pondering where Pedder's historical reflections might be situated in terms of the fight for space in the psychological therapies' marketplace, as discussed in the previous chapter. Pedder's own call to arms in fighting for space for psychoanalytical therapy is navigational rather than militaristic. He challenges any staid notions of orthodoxy when it comes to training, and draws attention to Freud's training analysis of Eitingon, which was after dinner and during walks, twice a week. Flexibility, fittedness, and a model of needs seem to be Peddar's mantra. Pedder also bemoans some of the fractures in the psychoanalytic movement, the distance between group analysis and psychoanalysis. He realizes these are troubled times, but he hopes that his account will reassure practitioners that the struggle for legitimacy is hardly new, and, indeed, once upon a time, it was indeed more bruising and bloody.

Time will, of course, tell, though the recent debate concentrated around especially cognitive–behaviour therapy (CBT) has taken the fight for market placement to the heart of commissioning and evidence-based practice. In the most significant policy initiative of recent times, Lord Layard led a £214 million programme of developments in talking therapies. Although the recognition of the need for more therapy is acknowledged, cognitive–behaviour therapy (CBT) has rather cornered the market in terms of new monies released for NHS workforce training. There was a missed opportunity for other therapeutic modalities to wrestle central monies their way. The ever-present challenge, as it was in Budapest, is that of locating in-depth thinking in a runaway world. When short-cut surface solutions are offered, or easy pharmaceuticals, more sophisticated and complex treatments suffer. Klein and Balint found that new lines of advance could succeed when targeted in less expected arenas, Klein in working with children and Balint working with general practitioners. The lesson we might take from Pedder's history is that psychotherapy is at its best when it is imaginative, fluid, and responsive to a troubled world. What appears to be most reassuring about Pedder's historical review is that the struggle to locate psychoanalytic thinking is a perennial battle. Returning to his axiom (mentioned in the Chapter Six commentary), there is, after all, "no such thing as peace time".

Lines of advance: increasing access to psychoanalytic therapy

W hen asked to give the second APP lecture, and then pressed for a title, my unconscious came to the rescue and into my mind swam the title of Freud's 1919 paper, "Lines of advance in psychoanalytic therapy", which I thought I could borrow and change in line with the title of our own Association. I half remembered Freud's paper as extraordinarily prescient. Re-reading the paper, and thinking further about this, did nothing to dispel the idea, but increased its appeal to me.

There have always been tensions between exponents of the pure gold of analysis and the needs of its wider applications. More flexible arrangements and boundaries are necessary if we are to spread psychoanalysis beyond London and to fulfil Freud's own hopes about the large-scale application of psychoanalytic therapy. Freud's (1919a) paper; "Lines of advance in psychoanalysis", is taken as a starting-point to review how far we have advanced towards fulfilment of his prophetic remarks about the need to develop psychoanalytic psychotherapy for the masses. With its military implications, "lines of advance", which is a sort of rallying cry, "onward, analytic soldiers", a glance is taken back to some of the circumstances and characters involved in Budapest, where the paper was given at the 1918 congress, where there was much talk about the need also to do something about war neuroses.

It is now more than seventy years, or a life-span, since the publication of Freud's (1919a) paper, which was published twenty years before Freud's death. When we are struggling where we work, in the NHS or other institutional settings, with day-to-day battles over cuts in resources, failing to get financed our latest hopes, or failing to get established as readily as we would like developments such as in academic psychotherapy, it is easy to be downhearted. I have always rather liked reading those interviews, or reviews, by retired or elderly psychiatrists and psychoanalysts who, in looking back over a professional life-time, can show us that things have changed for the better from the days when disturbed patients cowered in the back wards of mental hospitals. So, I thought it would be worth looking at what has changed since 1919, in those days in Budapest, with Melanie Klein, Ernest Jones, Michael Balint, and Sandor Ferenczi, where Freud's paper was first delivered.

Freud's 1919 paper is, in part, so prophetic and relevant that I did wonder mischievously how far I could get before you began to protest if I merely re-read his paper. Let me risk the first few paragraphs, with some editing or condensation.

> We have never prided ourselves on the completeness and finality of our knowledge and capacity. We are just as ready now as we were earlier to admit the imperfections of our understanding, to learn new things and to alter our methods in any way that can improve them . . . Now that we are met together . . . I feel drawn to review the position of our therapeutic procedure . . . and to take a survey of the new directions in which it may develop. [Freud, 1919a, p. 159]

He goes on to defend the use of the expression "analysis", criticized by some as implying too dismantling a procedure, and for not giving sufficient attention to the subsequent necessary resynthesis. He expresses a cautionary note about Ferenczi's "active" technique, but only after introducing it by saying,

> Developments in our therapy, therefore, will no doubt proceed along other lines; first and foremost, along the one which Ferenczi . . . has lately termed "activity" on the part of the analyst. You will

observe that this opens up a new field of analytic technique the working over of which will require close application and which will lead to quite definite rules of procedure. [*ibid.*, p. 162]

He acknowledges that for some patients:

One has to combine analytic with educative influence; and even with the majority, occasions now and then arise in which the physician is bound to take up the position of teacher and mentor. But it must always be done with great caution, and the patient should be educated to liberate and fulfil his own nature, not to resemble ourselves. [*ibid.*, p. 165]

It is not exactly clear what Freud means here by "educative influence". But one could see a line of advance, or developmental line, stretching forward to group therapy and family therapy, with more of an emphasis on the therapist as a role model. He is more definite in referring to the treatment of phobias, where patients may have to be encouraged to face the objects of their fear. As he says, "The phobias have already made it necessary for us to go beyond our former limits. One can hardly master a phobia if one waits till the patient lets the analysis influence him to give it up" (*ibid.*, p. l65).

Here, a line stretches forward to more modern treatments, such as guided mourning, where patients are exposed to painful or avoided memories, or encouraged to visit the cemetery, or look at photographs of the deceased, or to ways of handling perinatal bereavement (Bourne & Lewis, 1984). Freud concludes the paper by casting a glance to the future and to the spread of psychotherapy to the population at large. I will return to that conclusion later, to try to see how far Freud's predictions have been fulfilled.

But first, let us consider the circumstances in which the paper published in 1919 was composed and given, which was at the Fifth International Psychoanalytic Congress held in Budapest in September 1918. In 1918, Freud was sixty-two, an age at which he had long imagined he might die, confirmed, he thought, when six and two were the last two figures of the telephone number allotted him (Gay, 1988). Perhaps feeling his age, this was the first time he read a paper rather than speaking, as usual, without even any notes. He had written the paper while staying with the family of

Anton von Freund in Hungary, at the beginning of his summer holiday on the way to Budapest. In September 1918, the First World War still had two months to run, until the Armistice in November. The moving spirit for holding the Congress before the end of the war was Abraham. Ernest Jones (1955) tells us "it was at first planned to hold it in Breslau, but at the beginning of September it was decided to change to Budapest, which Freud now declared to be the 'centre of the psychoanalytical movement'" (p. 222).

Jones writes that because of the war, it could not be truly international, but it was subsequently agreed to give it official status as the Fifth International Psychoanalytic Congress (5th IPA). It was the first Congress at which official representatives of any government were present, in this case of the Austrian, German, and Hungarian governments. The reason for their attendance was the increasing appreciation of the part played by war neuroses, which, together with the work of Abraham, Eitingon, and Ferenczi, had made an impression on high-ranking Army medical officers, and there was talk of establishing psychoanalytic clinics at various centres for the treatment of war neuroses. Similar pressures led to the founding of the Tavistock Clinic and Cassel Hospital, as well as to the opening of the Maudsley Hospital, as we saw in the previous chapter.

The first such clinic was to have been in Budapest. The benefactor was to be Anton von Freund, whose family Freud had stayed with that summer on the way to Budapest. As yet, there was no realization of the imminent outcome of the war, which changed the whole situation. Anton von Freund was born in Budapest in 1880. He got a doctorate in philosophy, but entered the family brewing business. He had had a sarcoma of the testicle removed, but apprehension about recurrences precipitated a neurosis, for which Freud treated him. Freund became interested in psychoanalysis, and was disposed to philanthropic plans for disposing of his fortune and devoting it to the furtherance of psychoanalysis. The idea was conceived of founding a psychoanalytic institute and clinic in Budapest, as well as an independent psychoanalytic publishing firm. At first, the idea was to establish the latter in Budapest, where the money was, but, after the war, Freud insisted the publishing house should be in Vienna.

Balint (1947) said von Freund was "perhaps the most lovable man in the early history of psychoanalysis". He became secretary of the IPA at the Budapest Congress, but died, only two years later, in 1920. Freud (1920c) wrote in his obituary:

> The great success he attained as a manufacturer and organiser failed to satisfy the two needs which were active in the depths of his nature—for social benefaction and scientific activity . . . When, during his last years, he came to know psychoanalysis, it seemed to him to promise the fulfilment of his two great wishes. He set himself the task of helping the masses by psychoanalysis . . . to mitigate the neurotic suffering of the poor. Since the State took no heed of the neuroses of the common people, since hospital clinics for the most part rejected psychoanalytic therapy . . . Anton von Freund sought, by his private initiative, to open a path for every one towards the fulfilment of this important social duty. During the years of the war he had collected what was then a very considerable sum . . . for humanitarian purposes in the city of Budapest. . . . He assigned this sum for the foundation of a psychoanalytic institute in Budapest . . . of which Ferenczi was to be the scientific head . . . and the founder handed over a relatively smaller sum to Professor Freud for the foundation of an international psychoanalytic publishing house . . . Von Freund's premature death has put an end to these philanthropic schemes, with all their scientific hopes. . . . None the less, the example which von Freund sought to set has already had its effect. A few weeks after his death, thanks to the energy and liberality of Max Eitingon [a rich Russian analyst] the first psychoanalytic outpatients clinic has been opened in Berlin. [pp. 267–268]

The Congress was held in the Hotel Gellert, in Budapest. As we have already seen, Freud began his paper by justifying his use of the word "analysis" and then expressed reservations about Ferenczi's active technique, though acknowledging the necessity in phobias. He then, in Ernest Jones' (1955) words,

> concluded by envisaging the future when the State would take serious cognizance of the cost and the vast amount of suffering and inefficiency resulting from neuroses, transcending that, for instance, caused by tuberculosis, and would take the same responsibility for the treatment of poor patients as is done with other disorders. Now, thirty-five years later, there are slight indications of moves in this direction in Britain . . . [Jones, 1955, p. 268]

Freud's (1919a) own words in conclusion do bear quoting at some length:

And now in conclusion I will cast a glance at a situation which belongs to the future . . . Compared to the vast amount of neurotic misery which there is in the world, and perhaps need not be, the quantity we can do away with is almost negligible . . . Now let us assume that by some kind of organisation we succeeded in increasing our numbers to an extent sufficient for treating a considerable mass of the population. On the other hand, it is possible to foresee that at some time or other the conscience of society will awake and remind it that the poor man should have just as much right to assistance for his mind as he now has to the life-saving help offered by surgery; and that the neuroses threaten public health no less than tuberculosis. . . . When this happens, institutions or out-patient clinics will be started, to which analytically-trained physicians will be appointed. . . . Such treatments will be free. It may be a long time before the State comes to see these duties as urgent . . . Probably these institutions will first be started by private charity. Some time or other, however, it must come to this. We shall then be faced by the task of adapting our technique to the new conditions. . . . We shall need to look for the simplest and most easily intelligible ways of expressing our theoretical doctrines . . . It is very probable, too, that the large-scale application of our therapy will compel us to alloy the pure gold of analysis freely with the copper of direct suggestion; and hypnotic influence, too, might find a place in it again as it has in the treatment of war neuroses. [pp. 166–168]

The war neuroses were at the front of every one's mind at the Congress, which also included a symposium on the Psychoanalysis of War Neuroses, with papers by Ferenczi, Abraham, and Simmel. These three papers, together with another on the same topic, from the opposing side in the war and the opposite end of Europe, by Ernest Jones, which had been read in London before the Royal Society of Medicine in April 1918, were published a year later in a small volume with an introduction by Freud (1919d). This was the first volume to be issued by the newly founded *Internationaler Psychoanalytischer Verlag*, which Freud had started in Vienna with the money from von Freund's benefaction.

War neurosis was a subject, interestingly, to which Freud also returned in a memorandum he was asked to submit to a Commission set up by the Austrian War Ministry the following year

(1920) to investigate the ill-treatment of men suffering from war neuroses. This surfaced in the Archives of the Austrian War Ministry many years later and is also printed in the *Standard Edition* as an appendix to Freud's introduction to *Psychoanalysis and the War Neuroses* (1919d). Although Freud had declared Budapest to be the centre of the psychoanalytic movement, the final outcome of the war, and the revolutionary events in Hungary, altered all these hopes.

The tide of psychoanalysis began to flow westwards—to Berlin, Vienna, and London—but not before it had involved some central characters in Budapest, all of whom had an important influence on British psychoanalysis. I am thinking of Melanie Klein, Michael Balint, and Ernest Jones, all of whom were in analysis with Ferenczi.

Melanie Klein had moved with her husband, in 1910, to Budapest, where she first came across psychoanalytic ideas in 1914, reading a paper of Freud's, "On dreams". She probably attended meetings of the newly-formed Hungarian psychoanalytic society, founded by Ferenczi in 1914. She started analysis in Budapest with Ferenczi, who first suggested the idea of analysis of children to her. She presented a paper on child analysis to the Hungarian Society, following which she was immediately made a member. This paper was about the analysis of her son, Eric. Melanie Klein first saw Freud reading his Budapest Congress paper in 1918. She moved to Berlin in 1921, where she re-contacted Abraham, whom she had first met at the 1920 Psychoanalytic Congress. He further encouraged her attempts at the psychoanalysis of children. In 1924, she entered analysis with Abraham, but he died the following year while she first came to London to lecture on child analysis, arranged through the Stracheys and Ernest Jones. The next year, in 1926, she settled in London.

Ernest Jones, who had been in Canada for several years, spent the summer and autumn of 1913 in Budapest, on the advice of Freud, being analysed by Ferenczi, for an hour twice a day, perhaps even at the same time as Klein (Grosskurth [1985] suggests). Ernest Jones returned to London to found the London Psycho-Analytical Society in 1913, though he later dissolved it, and re-founded it as the British Psychoanalytical Society in 1919. If political upheavals drove psychoanalysis westwards from Budapest, and later on from

Berlin to London and the USA, then their loss has been our gain. It is a sad and ironic comment on human affairs that disasters and tragedies also lead to all kinds of social progress and invention.

The First World War increased interest in neurotic, non-psychotic disorders, otherwise known as functional disorders, or shell-shock. We have already seen this interest in the 1918 Budapest Congress, though, because of the outcome of events, this did not produce the clinics that Freud had hoped for in Budapest. However, a similar interest in Berlin led to the founding of the first psychoanalytic outpatient clinic there in 1920, founded by Eitingon, who had his analysis in after-dinner walks with Freud. It was under this same impetus that soon after the War the Tavistock Clinic and Cassel Hospital were founded. The Maudsley Hospital was opened for similar reasons, though it was believed at the Maudsley that such cases were due to punctuate brain haemorrhages, a view later retracted by Mott, according to Dicks (1970), when he acknowledged that the majority were psychogenic.

Advances after the Second World War

Similarly, in the Second World War, there was a further acceleration of interest in psychodynamic and psychoanalytic ideas. The names of Bion, Foulkes, and Main are well known, and their work in army psychiatry, and in the Northfields Experiment, which led to developments in group psychotherapy and in therapeutic community ideas. It is, perhaps, of relevant interest that high profile psychoanalysts and psychotherapists have taken part in movements for the prevention of nuclear war. Short of outright war, I wonder if we are not seeing a surge of interest in analytic ideas in response to disasters, such as Zeebrugge, Kings Cross, and others, in which psychotherapists have been involved in developing post trauma treatments. Psychoanalysts are good at keeping their torch alight, but have not always been so good at offering its warmth to outsiders. It has often been the pressure of external events that has dragged them from their lairs or prompted others to turn to them for help.

Another different line of advance could be traced from the history of psychoanalytic publications. *The Internationaler Psychoanalytischer Verlag*, financed by von Freund, started in Vienna, and

Freud always took a close interest in it himself. I have already said that the first volume was on *Psychoanalysis and the War Neuroses*, with Freud's own introduction. It continued until it was closed by the Nazis after the Anschluss in 1938. Fortunately, an English branch had been started by Ernest Jones, and continued as the International Psycho-Analytical Library, forces being joined between the Hogarth Press and the Institute of Psycho-Analysis to publish both the International Psycho-Analytical Library and the *Standard Edition*. Recently, the New Library of Psychoanalysis has started in conjunction with Tavistock Publications, and finds itself in some competition with Free Association Books, an example of how psychoanalytic energies and creative forces have broken out beyond the bounds of their established and, perhaps, too conservative organizations.

In the development of psychoanalytic treatments in the public sphere, institutions have had an integral role. Tensions between the pure gold of analysis and its applications have always been a problem, or tensions between centres of excellence, such as the Institute of Psycho-Analysis and the Tavistock, and others with fewer resources. I see psychoanalysis as the central lighthouse that illuminates and informs all other forms of analytic psychotherapy, and by the light of which dynamic psychotherapists, in varying craft, navigate at varying distances from the rock on which the lighthouse stands. We need both devoted lighthouse keepers and rough-and-ready sailors prepared to explore into strange waters. Too often, they tend to polarize and scorn each other, failing to recognize that each depends on and needs the other.

The Association for Psychoanalytic Psychotherapy (APP) inhabits the borderland between centre and periphery, the rocks and the seas. It was, indeed, set up for the very purpose of doing something about improvements in the delivery of psychoanalytic therapy in the public sphere. Freud's remark at the end of his 1919 paper bears repeating and pondering: "the large-scale application of our therapy will compel us to alloy the pure gold of analysis freely with the copper of direct suggestion". Analytic purists might easily take this to mean that Freud thought gold inevitably superior to copper. But remember his familiarity with the "Three Caskets" scenes in Shakespeare's *The Merchant of Venice*, and his use of it as an illustration of parapraxes. Portia was bound by her father's will to give her hand to whichever of the three suitors chose correctly one of the three caskets of gold, silver and lead. The princely suitors confidently go for gold and silver, and are dismissed empty-handed. As Bassanio, Portia's favourite, makes his choice she betrays her wish in a slip, which Freud quotes in the *Psychopathology of Everyday Life* and in his *Introductory Lectures* (Freud, 1916–1917).

> I pray you tarry; pause a day or two
> Before you hazard . . .
> . . . I could teach you
> How to choose right, but then I am forsworn;
> . . . One half of me is yours, the other half yours,—
> Mine own, I would say; but if mine, then yours, And so all yours.

So, maybe Freud would have agreed with the note inside the gold casket that "All that glisters is not gold". One of our problems in furthering lines of advance is in moving the influence of psychoanalysis and psychoanalytic psychotherapy beyond London. A very few psychoanalysts have practised entirely independently beyond London; most have had an institutional base, often as consultant psychotherapist. Of a hundred consultant psychotherapists in the NHS in 1990, about half were psychoanalysts, most in London were, and most beyond London were not. Steps have been taken by the British Psycho-Analytical Society to try to do something about psychoanalysis beyond London, and links have been developed with graduates of the Scottish Institute of Human Relations. I have always thought that a central problem has been too rigid an adherence to the fixed Gold Standard of five times a week psychoanalysis. It is at least worth thinking of going off the Gold Standard, and settling for a more flexible rate, which might be at around three to four times a week. I think the British Psycho-Analytical Society has been too conservative over this, and it has contributed to the difficulty of psychoanalysis not moving far beyond London.

There are other psychoanalytic associations round the world who train on a three or four times a week basis. Three times a week is the commonest modality in the analytic psychotherapy trainings in the UK, those that are represented in the Analytic Psychotherapy group in the new United Kingdom Standing Conference for Psychotherapy, which has emerged out of the Rugby Conferences through the 1980s. The British Psycho-Analytical Society still sticks to a five times a week basis of training; the Society of Analytical Psychology (SAP) and Scottish Institute of Human Relations, four times a week; child psychotherapists, the ACP suggest three to five times a week; but most other trainings are all three times a week: British Association of Psychotherapists, Arbours, Lincoln, London Centre for Psychotherapy, Severnside, and the Tavistock four-year course. Less is demanded in Diploma and MSc courses in psychotherapy, which, over the past ten years, have sprung up more in centres beyond London: most require their trainees to attend a weekly sensitivity group (Pedder, 1989). Where they require individual psychotherapy, it is usually on a once a week basis, outside London. An interesting question to ask is whether provincial courses will repeat the history of psychoanalytic training, which was not always three to five times a week.

Another line of advance could be seen in the developments which were traced by Balint (1953) in an article on "Analytic training and training analysis":

The greatest mistake we could make would be to consider our present training system as a final or even settled solution. . . . The present system is only one more step in a long development, after many previous steps have been found faulty in one respect or another. [p. 275]

It is again worth remembering Freud's opening words in 1919: ". . . we have never prided ourselves on the completeness and finality of our knowledge and capacity". Balint divides the history of training analysis into five periods:

The first period [1900–1910] was that of pure instruction, done mainly by the pupil himself almost without any help from outside, simply by reading Freud's books. Soon after, the need for something more than intellectual knowledge was recognized and that "something more" consisted of a short analysis lasting some weeks to some months, which enabled the candidate to experience in his own mind the validity and force of the main findings of psychoanalysis. [1953, p. 275]

The second period (1910–1920, or up to the Budapest Congress) Balint calls "the period of demonstration". I would like to quote a very early, perhaps the earliest, description the period of demonstration by Freud in a letter to Ferenczi, 22 October 1909: "Eitingon is here. Twice weekly, after dinner, he comes with me for a walk and has his analysis during it" (cited in Balint, 1953, p. 275). This was around 1910, when the International Psychoanalytical Association was founded, when Freud maintained that a self-analysis was indispensable for the practice of analysis, though he did not clarify whether he meant an analysis by oneself or another person. It was Jung who recommended, in 1919, that anyone who wished to carry out analyses on others should first undergo an analysis by someone with expert knowledge.

But it was only in 1922, at the International Psychoanalytic Association Congress in Berlin, that it was stipulated that a training analysis by somebody else was obligatory for any would-be analyst. Balint (1953) continued,

> The third period [1920–Second World War], that of "proper analysis" was able to establish itself only after heated debates ... The protagonist in the attack against the method of "demonstration" was Ferenczi, whose main argument ... was that it was an untenable situation that the patients should be better analysed than their analysts. [p. 276]

It seems a fair way of putting it. He demanded that a training analysis should last about as long, and should go about as deep, as a therapeutic analysis. At that time, the 1920s, it was thought it should be one-and-a-half to two years, but,

> the problem was forgotten, and the next, the fourth, period started by the acceptance of another, still more exacting, demand, also by Ferenczi, according to which training analyses should achieve more than therapeutic analyses. [*ibid.*]

Then, from 1947 onwards, the training period became four years, until a fifth period, or what Balint calls the period of "supertherapy", when analyses got even longer—to five or ten years. Has this line of advance towards five times a week training gone too far towards gold?

Waves of advance

How will psychotherapy services fare in the future? What will be the major historical force to influence events, as the two world wars did? Might it be time for a new English Reformation? What will be the effect of the development of internal markets in the NHS? Will there be a contracting out of services, a privatization of psychotherapy, so to speak? Will the frameworks for community care, as suggested initially in the Griffiths report, have adequately funded service provision, or will the pressures under which social service departments operate allow time and space only for "life-and-limb" emergencies? There are risks here for both adult and child psychotherapy services. What will be the effect of European integration? Presumably, psychoanalysts trained on a three times a week basis in France will certainly be entitled to come here and call themselves psychoanalysts. Why will the BAP training stand in any less regard at such a time? The training of their Jungian stream has already been accepted by their international organization.

Discussions continue at the United Kingdom Standing Conference for Psychotherapy on these issues, of registration, and of the place of the core professions. Should entry to the regulated practice and profession of psychotherapy be via the core professions, as in Holland, or should we promote more radical solutions? If via the core profession, should these be psychiatry, psychology, and social work? Or should others, such as nursing, be included, or teaching, which is relevant to child therapy training?

All this is relevant to the emergence of a new profession of non-medical adult psychotherapist. It is becoming clear that, *de facto*, a new discipline of adult psychotherapist (non-medical) has emerged within the NHS. Initially, there were about twenty such posts in London, at Willesden and the Portman Clinic, and then outside London in Nottingham, Portsmouth, and Lincoln. Some radicals in these positions wanted instant parity in all respects with medical psychotherapists, and wanted to drop the "non-medical" tag. Others, perhaps reactionaries too, resisted the development at all.

I think it is worth looking, briefly, at the history of the development of child psychotherapists, since their history, very interestingly, parallels the development of this possible new profession of adult non-medical psychotherapists. 1989 was the fortieth year of the Association of Child Psychotherapists (ACP) (Lush, 1989), the umbrella organization which scrutinizes and oversees the various training courses in child psychotherapy. Child psychotherapy began in England before the War, with Melanie Klein's arrival to lecture in 1925 and her work from 1926 onwards, and then Anna Freud's arrival in the late 1930s. Discussions on training were delayed by the War. Some doctors did not approve of the idea of lay psychotherapists at all—though Freud and Ferenczi had always been in favour of lay analysis, by contrast to the early situation in America. Some psychologists did not see the need of such a new profession. It was, however, facilitated by Bowlby, and, in 1949, the first two trainings started: inside the NHS, at the Tavistock Clinic, supported by Bowlby, and outside the NHS at Anna Freud's Hampstead Clinic.

At first it was called the Provisional Association of Child Psychotherapists (Non-Medical), the "non-medical" put there at the insistence of the medical profession. The provisional association had a medical advisory council and the training council had to have equal numbers of medical and non-medical members. In 1951, they dropped "provisional" from the title. In 1972, they dropped "non-medical" from the title, and in 1977, they dropped their medical advisory council.

The development of the non-medical psychotherapy, child and adult, would seem to be an example of the waves of advance in psychotherapy. Borrowing a metaphor from the wave machine in the swimming-pool of the Hotel Gellert in Budapest, we could think of waves of advance as well as clear lines of advance. There have been the successive waves of pressure of the two World Wars, and I have suggested the next waves will be National Health Service changes and the effects of entering Europe.

Balint (1968) in *The Basic Fault*, in a chapter on classical technique and its limitations, addressed the problem of pure gold and copper. Intimately connected with this problem is the question whose task it should be to devise the "other", non-classical and yet dynamic, psychotherapies that might then be used in the case of patients declared unsuitable for "classical analysis";

Should this task be surrendered to "wild" analysts, to eclectics, to general psychiatrists—or perhaps to faith healers? It is well worth remembering that on one occasion in our past we did not hesitate at all to extend our scope well beyond the confines of "classical" technique. This was the case of child analysis, for which new techniques had to be developed to meet a new therapeutic situation. . . . Despite such fundamental differences we did not surrender child analysis to, say, the educational psychologists, but shouldered the problem ourselves. Since then child analysis has been a specialized study, but none the less an integral part of the body of psychoanalysis.

It will be an intriguing historical—and psychological study to find out what prompted psychoanalytic opinion to adopt exactly the opposite attitude in the case of group therapy. Although Freud himself adumbrated some alloying of the pure gold of psychoanalysis in order to make it suitable for the psychotherapy of the broad masses, and although almost all of the pioneers of group therapy were trained psychoanalysts, we, as a body, refused to accept responsibility for its further development—in my opinion, to the detriment of everyone concerned, above all of our own science. [*ibid.*, pp. 101–102]

I used to wonder, like Balint, why group analysis, like child analysis, had not remained more closely within the family of psychoanalysis; but then, when in turn family therapy broke away from group analysis and founded its own separate institute and journal, a pattern of generational separation and individuation became clearer. What will be the next wave of advance in this sense? Will it be towards briefer therapies backed by economic pressures? We would then need to stick even more firmly to our conviction that, for training purposes at least, more extensive analytic experience is necessary; for, to quote Freud's (1919a) final words:

whatever form this psychotherapy for the people may take, whatever the elements out of which it is compounded, its most effective and most important ingredients will assuredly remain those borrowed from strict and untendentious psychoanalysis. [p. 168]

How far would Freud feel we had fulfilled his 1919 predictions, as he looks out from his statue at Swiss Cottage to the present site of the Tavistock Clinic, which followed him to the foothills of

Hampstead? Having had hopes, in 1919, of Budapest becoming the centre of psychoanalysis, living in England in 1939, he complimented Ernest Jones that "the events of recent years have made London the site and centre of the psychoanalytic movement". This was certainly true of the post-war years, and, in many ways, still is; for example, the numbers attracted to train here from abroad, the demand for speakers and supervisors from all round the country and abroad. But the British Psycho-Analytical Society remains fairly static in size, certainly by comparison with the growth of many other European societies. I imagine Freud might think it has become a bit too inflexible to respond to the needs of the poor he foresaw in the conclusion to his 1919 paper. Other psychotherapy trainings and regional courses have sprung up to meet these needs. Balint (1947) commented on Freud's 1919a paper:

> The original idea clearly delineated by Freud: psychotherapy for the masses, became completely lost in the years of development. It is a justified charge against us analysts that we are so little concerned about it, and only a fair consequence that the therapy of the masses is passing more and more into other hands and will eventually be solved—rightly or wrongly—without us. [p. 263]

I want to end with a plea for a measure of flexibility in our arrangements: not a return to the days of Eitingon and his twice-weekly after-dinner analysis with Freud, but to remember Ernest Jones's two hours a day analysis and the flexibility needed to help those beyond London, as the Tavistock end-of-week course is now doing. If any scorn these developments as copper, let them remember the caskets, and Freud's own words, "The large-scale application, of our therapy will compel us to alloy the pure gold of analysis with the copper of direct suggestion".

REFERENCES

Abraham, K. (1924). A short study of the development of the libido. In: E. Jones (Ed.), *Selected Papers on Psychoanalysis*. London: Hogarth Press, 1927.

Abse, W. (1974). *Clinical Notes on Group-Analytic Psychotherapy*. Bristol: Wright.

Alexander, F. (1957). *Psychoanalysis and Psychotherapy*. London: Allen & Unwin.

Balint, E. (1976). Psychoanalysis applied to medicine: a personal note. *International Journal of Psychiatry in Medicine, 7*: 35–46.

Balint, E., & Norell, J. S. (1973). *Six Minutes for the Patient*. London: Tavistock.

Balint, M. (1937). Early developmental states of the ego—primary object-love. In: *Primary Love and Psychoanalytic Technique*. London: Tavistock, 1965.

Balint, M. (1947). On the psychoanalytic training system. In: *Primary Love and Psychoanalytic Technique*. London: Tavistock, 1965.

Balint, M. (1950a). Changing therapeutical aims and techniques in a psycho-analysis. *International Journal of Psychoanalysis, 31*: 117–124.

Balint, M. (1950b). On the termination of analysis. *International Journal of Psychoanalysis, 31*: 196–199.

Balint, M. (1952). New beginning and the paranoid and the depressive syndromes. In: *Primary Love and Psychoanalytic Technique*. London: Tavistock, 1965.

Balint, M. (1953). Analytic training and training analysis. In: *Primary Love and Psychoanalytic Technique*. London: Tavistock, 1965.

Balint, M. (1957). *The Doctor, His Patient and the Illness*. London: Pitman.

Balint, M. (1965). *Primary Love and Psychoanalytic Technique*. London: Tavistock.

Balint, M. (1968). *The Basic Fault*. London: Tavistock.

Balint, M., & Balint, E. (1961). *Psychotherapeutic Techniques in Medicine*. London: Tavistock.

Bibring, E. (1953). The mechanism of depression. In: P. Greenacre (Ed.), *Affective Disorders*. New York: International Universities Press.

Bion, W. R. (1961). *Experiences in Groups*. London: Tavistock.

Birtchnell, J. (1984). Dependence and its relation to depression. *British Journal of Medical Psychology, 57*: 215–225.

Birtchnell, J. (1988). Defining dependence. *British Journal of Medical Psychology, 61*: 111–123.

Bloch, S. (1979). *An Introduction to the Psychotherapies*. Oxford: Oxford University Press.

Bollas, C. (1987). Ordinary regression to dependence. In: *The Shadow of the Object*. London: Free Association Books.

Bourne, S., & Lewis, F. (1984). Pregnancy after stillbirth or neonatal death. *Lancet, 2*: 31–33.

Bowlby, J. (1958). The nature of the child's tie to his mother: In: *Attachment and Loss, Vol. I* (appendix) London: Hogarth Press, 1969.

Bowlby, J. (1969). *Attachment and Loss. Vol. I: Attachment*. London: Hogarth Press.

Bowlby, J. (1973). *Attachment and Loss. Vol. II: Separation: Anxiety & Anger*. London: Hogarth Press.

Bowlby, J. (1980). *Attachment and Loss. Vol. III: Loss, Sadness & Depression*. London: Hogarth Press.

Breuer, J., & Freud, S. (1895d). *Studies on Hysteria. S.E., 2*. London: Hogarth.

British Medical Journal (1988). W. W. Sargant. Obituary. 297, 789–90.

Brown, D., & Pedder, J. (1979). *Introduction to Psychotherapy*. London: Tavistock (2nd edition, Routledge, 1991).

Brown, G. W., & Harris, T. (1978a). *Social Origins of Depression*. London: Tavistock.

Brown, G. W., & Harris, T. (1978b). Social origins of depression: a reply. *Psychological Medicines, 8*: 577–588.

Burnett, F. H. (1911). *The Secret Garden*. London: Heinemann.

Buxbaum, E. (1950). Technique of terminating analysis. *International Journal of Psychoanalysis, 31*: 184–190.

Cawley, R. H. (1977). The teaching of psychotherapy. *AUTP Newsletter, January*: 19–36.

Dare, C., & Holder, A. (1981). Developmental aspects of the interaction between narcissism, self-esteem and object relations. *International Journal of Psycho-Analysis, 62*: 323–337.

Dewald, P. A. (1966). Forced termination of psychoanalysis. *Bulletin of the Menninger Clinic, 30*: 98–110.

Dewald, P. A. (1982). The clinical importance of the termination phase. *Psychoanalytic Inquiry, 2*: 441–461.

Dicks, H. V. (1970). *Fifty Years of the Tavistock Clinic*. London: Routledge.

Doi, T. (1962). Amae—a key concept for understanding Japanese personality structure. In: R. J. Smith & R. K. Beardsley (Eds), *Japanese Culture*. Chicago, IL: Aldine.

Doi, T. (1973). *The Anatomy of Dependence*. Tokyo: Kodnnska International.

Doi, T. (1989). The concept of ama, and its psychoanalytic implications. *International Review of Psycho-Analysis, 16*: 349–354.

Eliot, T. S. (1943). *Four Quartets*. London: Faber & Faber.

Ellenberger, H. F. (1970). *The Discovery of the Unconscious*. London: Allen Lane.

Engel, G. L. (1971). Attachment behaviour, object relations and the dynamic–economic points of view. *International Journal of Psychoanalysis, 52*: 183–196.

Erikson, E. H. (1980). On the generational cycle. *International Journal of Psychoanalysis, 61*: 213-223.

Fairbairn, W. R. D. (1952). *Psychoanalytic Studies of the Personality*. London: Tavistock.

Ferenczi, S. (1927). The problem of the termination of the analysis. In: *Final Contributions*. London: Hogarth, 1955.

Ferenczi, S. (1952). *Further Contributions to the Theory and Technique of Psycho-Analysis*. London: Hogarth.

Firestein, S. K. (1974). Termination of psychoanalysis of adults: a review of the literature. *Journal of the American Psychoanalytic Association, 22*: 873–894.

Firestein, S. K. (1978). *Termination in Psychoanalysis*. New York: International University Press.

Firestein, S. K. (1982). Termination of psychoanalysis: theoretical, clinical and pedagogic considerations. *Psychoanalytic Inquiry, 2*: 473–497.

Fleming, J. (1967). Teaching the basic skills of psychotherapy. *Archives of General Psychiatry*, 16: 416–426.

Fordham, M. (1978). *Jungian Psychotherapy: A Study in Analytical Psychology*. Chichester: Wiley.

Forster, E. M. (1910). *Howard's End*. London: Arnold.

Foulkes, S. H. (1964). *Therapeutic Group Analysis*. London: Allen & Unwin.

Freud, A. (1936). *The Ego and the Mechanisms of Defence*. London: Hogarth Press, 1966.

Freud, A. (1980). *Normality and Pathology in Childhood*. London: Hogarth.

Freud, S. (1894a). The neuro-psychoses of defence. *S.E.*, 3: 45–69. London: Hogarth.

Freud, S. (1900a). *The Interpretation of Dreams*. *S.E.*, 4–5. London: Hogarth.

Freud, S. (1905e). *Fragment of an Analysis of a Case of Hysteria*. *S.E.*, 7: 7–123. London: Hogarth.

Freud, S. (1912e). Recommendations to physicians practising psychoanalysis. *S.E.*, 12: 109–120. London: Hogarth.

Freud, S. (1914c). On narcissism: an introduction. *S.E.*, 14: 73–102. London: Hogarth.

Freud, S. (1915a). Observations on transference-love. *S.E.*, 12: 157–174. London: Hogarth.

Freud, S. (1916–1917). *Introductory Lectures on Psycho-Analysis*. *S.E.*, 15–16. London: Hogarth.

Freud, S. (1917b). Mourning and melancholia. *S.E.*, 14: 243–258. London: Hogarth.

Freud, S. (1919a). Lines of advance in psychoanalytic therapy. *S.E.*, 17: 157–168. London: Hogarth.

Freud, S. (1919g). Preface to Reik's "Ritual: Psychoanalytic Studies". *S.E.*, 17: 257–264. London: Hogarth.

Freud, S. (1919d). Introduction to *Psycho-analysis and the War Neuroses*. *S.E.*, 17: 205–216. London: Hogarth.

Freud, S. (1920c). Dr Anton von Freund. *S.E.*, 18: 267–268. London: Hogarth.

Freud, S. (1923b). *The Ego and the Id*. *S.E.*, 19: 3–66. London: Hogarth.

Freud, S. (1926e). The question of lay analysis. *S.E.*, 20: 183–258. London: Hogarth.

Freud, S. (1937c). Analysis terminable and interminable. *S.E.*, 23: 209–254. London: Hogarth.

Frijling-Schreuder, E. C. M. (1970). On individual supervision. *International Journal of Psycho-Analysis*, 51: 363–370.

Furman, E. (1974). *A Child's Parent Dies*. New Haven, CT: Yale University Press.

Gask, L., & McGrath, G. (1989). Psychotherapy and general practice. *British Journal of Psychiatry, 154*: 445–453.

Gaskill, H. S. (1980). The closing phase of the psychoanalytic treatment of adults and the goals of psychoanalysis: 'The myth of perfectibility'. *International Journal of Psychoanalysis, 61*: 11–23.

Gay, P. (1988). *Freud: a Life for Our Time*. London: Dent.

Glover, E. (1955). *The Technique of Psychoanalysis*. New York: International Universities Press.

Greenson, R. R. (1965). The working alliance and the transference neurosis. *Psychoanalytic Quarterly, 34*: 155–181.

Greenson, R. R. (1967). *The Technique and Practice of Psychoanalysis*. London: Hogarth.

Grinberg, L. (1980). The closing phase of the psychoanalytic treatment of adults and the goals of psychoanalysis: "the search for truth about oneself". *International Journal of Psychoanalysis, 61*: 25–37.

Grosskurth, P. (1985). *Melanie Klein*. London: Hodder & Stoughton.

Guntrip, H. (1961). *Personality Structure and Human Interaction*. London: Hogarth.

Hamilton, J. W. (1976). Early trauma, dreaming and creativity: the works of Eugene O'Neill. *International Review of Psycho-Analysis, 3*: 341–364.

Hayman, A. (1974). Muddles and metaphors (paper read to British Psychoanalytical Society; unpublished).

Heimann, P. (1950). On counter-transference. *International Journal of Psycho-Analysis, 31*: 81–84.

Hill, D. (1982). In conversation with Sir Denis Hill, Part II. *Bulletin of the Royal College of Psychiatrists, 6*(6): 94–97.

Jacobson, E. (1964). *The Self and the Object World*. New York: International Universities Press.

Jaques, E. (1965). Death and the mid-life crisis. *International Journal of Psycho-Analysis, 46*: 502–514.

Joffe, W. G., & Sandler, J. (1965). Notes on pain, depression and individuation. *Psychoanalytic Study of the Child, 20*: 394–424.

Jones, E. (1910). The Oedipus complex as an explanation of Hamlet's mystery. *American Journal Psychology, 21*: 72–113.

Jones, E. (1936). The criteria of success in treatment. In: *Papers on Psycho-Analysis*. London: Maresfield Reprints, 1977.

Jones, E. (1949). *Hamlet and Oedipus*. London: Gollancz.

Jones, E. (1955). *Sigmund Freud: Life and Work, Vol. 2*. London: Hogarth.

Khan, M. M. R. (1969). On the clinical provision of frustrations, recognitions, and failures in the analytic situation. *International Journal of Psychoanalysis, 50*: 237–248.

Khan, M. M. R. (1970). Montaigne, Rousseau and Freud. In: *The Primacy of the Self*. London: Hogarth Press, 1974.

Khan, M. M. R. (1971). The role of illusion in the analytic space and process. In: *The Primacy of the Self*. London: Hogarth Press, 1974.

Khan, M. M. R. (1972a). On Freud's provision of the therapeutic frame. In: *The Primacy of the Self*. London: Hogarth Press, 1974.

Khan, M. M. R. (1972b). The finding and becoming of self. In: *The Primacy of the Self*. London: Hogarth, 1974.

Khan, M. M. R. (1972c). Dread of surrender to resourceless dependence in the analytic situation. In: *The Primacy of the Self*. London: Hogarth Press, 1974.

Khan, M. M. R. (1977). Secret as potential space. In: M. Tonnesmann & I. S. Kreeger (Eds), *Psychoanalysis and the Changing Society. Festschrift in Honour of Paula Heimann*. London: Tavistock.

Klauber, J. (1981). Analyses that cannot be terminated. In: *Difficulties in the Analytic Encounter*. London: Jason Aronson.

Klein, M. (1934). A contribution to the psychogenesis of manic-depressive states. In: *Contributions to Psychoanalysis*. London: Hogarth Press, 1948.

Klein, M. (1940). Mourning and its relation to manic–depressive states. In: *Contributions to Psycho-Analysis*. London: Hogarth Press, 1948.

Klein, M. (1950). On the criteria for the termination of a psychoanalysis. *International Journal of Psychoanalysis, 31*: 78–80.

Knights, L. C. (1974). Integration in the *Winter's Tale*. Paper read to Applied Section of the British Psychoanalytical Society; unpublished.

Langer, S. K. (1942). *Philosophy in a New Key*. Cambridge, MA: Harvard University Press.

Laplanche, J., & Pontalis, J. B. (1973). *The Language of Psycho-Analysis*. London: Hogarth.

Lebovici, S. (1970). Technical remarks on the supervision of psychoanalytic treatment. *International Journal of Psycho-Analysis, 51*: 385–392.

Lewis, A. J. (1934). The psychopathology of insight. In: *Inquiries in Psychiatry*. London: Routledge & Kegan Paul, 1967.

Lewis, A. J. (1967). Melancholia: a historical review. In: *The State of Psychiatry*. London: Routledge & Kegan Paul.

Lewis, C. S. (1966). *A Grief Observed*. London: Faber and Faber.

Lewis, E. (1976). The management of stillbirth: coping with an unreality. *The Lancet, 2*: 619–620.

Lieberman, S. (1978). Nineteen cases of morbid grief. *British Journal of Psychiatry, 132*: 159–163.

Limentani, A. (1982). On the "unexpected" termination of psychoanalytic therapy. *Psychoanalytic Inquiry, 2*: 419–440.

Little, M. (1960). On basic unity. *International Journal of Psychoanalysis, 41*: 377–384.

Loewald, H. W. (1962). Internalisation, separation, mourning and the superego. *Psychoanalytic Quarterly, 31*: 483–504.

Lorand, S. (1946). Termination. In: *Technique of Psychoanalytic Therapy*. New York: International Universities Press.

Lush, D. (1989). A short history of the Association of Child Psychotherapists. *Bulletin of ACP*, January.

Malan, D. H. (1963). *A Study of Brief Psychotherapy*. London: Tavistock.

Malan, D. H. (1979). *Individual Psychotherapy and the Science of Psychodynamics*. London: Butterworth.

Martindale, B. (1989). Becoming dependent again: the fears of some elderly persons and their younger therapists. *Psychoanalytic Psychotherapy, 4*: 67–75.

Matte Blanco, I. (1971). Book review of *Attachment and Loss, Vol. 1* by John Bowlby. *International Journal of Psychoanalysis, 52*: 197–199.

Mawson, D., Marks, I. M., Ramm, L., & Stern, R. S. (1981). Guided mourning for morbid grief: a controlled study. *British Journal of Psychiatry, 138*: 185–193.

Mendelson, M. (1974). *Psychoanalytic Concepts of Depression*. New York: Spectrum.

Milner, M. (1950). A note on the ending of an analysis. *International Journal of Psychoanalysis, 31*: 191–193.

Milner, M. (1971). *On Not Being Able to Paint*. London: Heinemann.

Neki, J. S. (1976). An examination of the cultural relativism of dependence as a dynamic of social and therapeutic relationships. *British Journal of Medical Psychology, 49*: 1–22.

Novick, J. (1982). Termination: themes and issues. *Psychoanalytic Inquiry, 2*: 329–365.

Ogden, T. H. (1979). On projective identification. *International Journal of Psychoanalysis, 60*: 357–373.

Panel (1963). Analysis terminable and interminable—twenty-five years later. *Journal of the American Psychoanalytic Association, 11*: 131–142.

Panel (1969). Problems of termination in the analysis of adults. *Journal of the American Psychoanalytic Association, 17*: 222–237.

Panel (1975). Termination: problems and techniques. *Journal of the American Psychoanalytic Association*, 23: 166–176.

Parkes, M. (1972). *Bereavement: Studies of Grief in Adult Life*. London: Tavistock.

Payne, S. (1950). Short communication on criteria for terminating analysis. *International Journal of Psychoanalysis*, 31: 205.

Pedder, J. R. (1977). The role of space and location in psychotherapy, play and theatre *International Journal of Psychoanalysis*, 4: 215–223.

Pedder, J. R. (1982). Failure to mourn, and melancholia. *British Journal of Psychiatry*, 141: 329–337.

Pedder, J. R. (1985). Loss and internalisation. *British Journal of Psychotherapy*, 1: 164–170.

Pedder, J. R. (1986). Reflections on the theory and practice of supervision. *Psychoanalytic Psychotherapy*, 2: 1–12.

Pedder, J. R. (1987). Some biographical contributions to psychoanalytic theories. *Free Associations*, 10: 12–16.

Pedder, J. R. (1989). Courses in psychotherapy: evolution and current trends. *British Journal of Psychotherapy*, 6: 203–221.

Pedder, J. R. (1990). Lines of advance in psychoanalytic psychotherapy. *Psychoanalytic Psychotherapy*, 4(3): 201–217.

Pines, M. (1974). Training in dynamic aspects of psychotherapy. In: V. Varma (Ed.), *Psychotherapy Today* (pp. 296–320). London: Constable.

Pirandello, L. (1921). *Six Characters in Search of an Author*. London: Heinemann, 1954.

Pontalis, J. B. (1974). Freud in Paris. *International Journal of Psychoanalysis*, 55: 455–458.

Ramsay, R. W. (1977). Behavioural approaches to bereavement. *Behaviour Research and Therapy*, 15: 131–135.

Reich, A. (1950). On the termination of analysis. *International Journal of Psychoanalysis*, 31: 179–183.

Richardson, K. (1989). Locally based community care. *Psychiatric Bulletin*, 13: 287–290.

Rickman, J. (1950). On the criteria for the termination of an analysis. *International Journal of Psychoanalysis*, 31: 200–201.

Rodman, F. R. (1986). *Keeping Hope Alive: On Becoming a Psychotherapist*. New York: Harper.

Royal College of Psychiatrists (1971). Guidelines for the training of general psychiatrists in psychotherapy. *British Journal of Psychiatry*, 119: 555–557.

Royal College of Psychiatrists (1991). The future of psychotherapy services. *Psychiatric Bulletin*, 15: 174–179.

Royal College of Psychiatrists (1993). Guidelines for psychotherapy training as part of general professional training. *Psychiatric Bulletin, 17*: 695–698.

Rycroft, C. (1962). Beyond the reality principle. *International Journal of Psychoanalysis, 43*: 388–394.

Rycroft, C. (1968). *A Critical Dictionary of Psychoanalysis*. London: Penguin, 1972.

Rycroft, C. (1985). *Psychoanalysis and Beyond*. London: Hogarth.

Schlessinger, N. (1966). Supervision of psychotherapy: a critical review of the literature. *Archives of General Psychiatry, 15*: 129–134.

Searles, H. F. (1955). The information value of the supervisor's emotional experiences. *Psychiatry, 18*: 135–146.

Segal, H. (1964). *Introduction to the Work of Melanie Klein*. London: Heinemann.

Shaffer, P. (1973). *Equus*. London: André Deutsch.

Sibbald, B., Addington-Hall, J., Brenneman, D., & Freeling, P. (1993). Counsellors in English and Welsh general practices: their nature mid distribution. *British Medical Journal, 306*: 29–33.

Siegel, B. L. (1982). Some thoughts on 'Some thoughts on termination', by Leo Rangell. *Psychoanalytic Inquiry, 2*: 393–398.

Sieghart, P. (1978). *Statutory Registration of Psychotherapists: Report of a Professions Joint Working Party*. Cambridge: Plumridge.

Silverman, J. S. (1971). Termination of analysis: graduation–initiation rite and mythopoetic aspects. In: M. Kanzer (Ed.), *The Unconscious Today* (pp. 288–305). New York: International University Press.

Solnit, A. J. (1970). Learning from psychoanalytic supervision. *International Journal of Psycho-Analysis, 51*: 359–362.

Storr, A. (1979). *The Art of Psychotherapy*. London: Heinemann.

Steiner, J. (1985). The training of psychotherapists. *Psychoanalytic Psychotherapy, 1*: 55–63.

Stephen, A. (1988). *The Suzy Lamplugh Story*. London: Faber.

Sutherland, J. D. (1968). The consultant psychotherapist in the NHS: his role and training. *British Journal of Psychiatry, 114*: 509–615.

Symington, N. (1986). *The Analytic Experience*. London: Free Association.

Tennant, C., & Bebbington, P. (1978). The social causation of depression: a critique of the work of Brown and his colleagues. *Psychological Medicine, 8*: 565–575.

Ticho, E. A. (1972). Termination of psychoanalysis: treatment goals, life goals. *Psychoanalytic Quarterly, 41*: 315–333.

Wilkinson, G. (1984). Psychotherapy in the market-place. *Psychological Medicine, 14*: 23–26.

Winnicott, C. (1978). D. W. W.: a reflection. In: S. A. Grolnick & L. Barkin (Eds), *Between Reality and Fantasy*. New York & London: Jason Aronson.

Winnicott, D. W. (1947). Hate in the countertransference. In: *Through Paediatrics to Psycho-Analysis*. London: Hogarth, 1975.

Winnicott, D. W. (1953). Transitional objects and transitional phenomena. In: *Playing and Reality*. London: Tavistock, 1971.

Winnicott, D. W. (1954). The depressive position in normal emotional development. In: *Through Paediatrics to Psychoanalysis*. London: Hogarth Press, 1975.

Winnicott, D. W. (1958). The capacity to be alone. In: *The Maturational Processes and the Facilitating Environment*. London: Hogarth Press, 1965.

Winnicott, D. W. (1959). Classification. In: *The Maturational Processes and the Facilitating Environment*. London: Hogarth Press.

Winnicott, D. W. (1960). Ego distortion in terms of true and false self. In: *The Maturational Processes and the Facilitating Environment*. London: Hogarth Press.

Winnicott, D. W. (1962). A personal view of the Kleinian contribution. In: *The Maturational Processes and the Facilitating Environment*. London: Hogarth Press, 1965.

Winnicott, D. W. (1963). The development of the capacity for concern. In: *The Maturational Processes and the Facilitating Environment*. London: Hogarth Press, 1965.

Winnicott, D. W. (1965). *The Maturational Processes and the Facilitating Environment*. London: Hogarth Press.

Winnicott, D. W. (1967a). Mirror-role of mother and family in child development. In: *Playing and Reality*. London: Tavistock, 1971.

Winnicott, D. W. (1967b). The location of cultural experience. In: *Playing and Reality*. London: Tavistock, 1971.

Winnicott, D. W. (1971). *Playing and Reality*. London: Tavistock.

Winnicott, D. W. (1975). *Through Paediatrics to Psychoanalysis*. London: Hogarth Press.

Wolff, H. H. (1971). The therapeutic and developmental functions of psychotherapy. *British Journal of Medical Psychology*, 44: 117–130.

Wright, K. J. T. (1976). Metaphor and symptom: a study of integration and its failure. *International Journal of Psychoanalysis*, 3: 97–109.

Zetzel, E. R. (1970). *The Capacity for Emotional Growth*. New York: International Universities Press.

INDEX